Tuscan Elements

First published in the United States in 2002 by

Watson-Guptill Publications

a division of VNU Business Media, Inc.

770 Broadway, New York, New York 10003

www.watsonguptill.com

Created by Co & Bear Productions (UK) Ltd.

Copyright © 2002 Co & Bear Productions(UK) Ltd.

Author Alexandra Black

Photographs copyright © 2002 Simon McBride

Manufactured in Italy

Publishers Beatrice Vincenzini & Francesco Venturi

Executive Director David Shannon

Editorial Director Alexandra Black

Art Director Pritty Ramjee

Designer Karen Watts

Publishing Assistant Ruth Deary

3 4 5 / 07 06 05

Library of Congress Control Number: 2002108602

ISBN: 0-8230-5480-2

Tuscan Elements

ALEXANDRA BLACK
Photography by Simon McBride

WATSON-GUPTILL PUBLICATIONS / NEW YORK

contents

stone 13

from the organic forms of field
stone to the precise lines of dressed
limestone and the smooth contours of
marble, this is the most fundamental
of Tuscan building materials.

wood 67

the golden hues of sun-baked clay
unify the vernacular architecture in the
form of terracotta tiles and bricks,
while glazed majolica brings colour
and artistry to the table.

earth 115

perpetuating the building traditions
of the ancient Etruscans, architectural
elements and furniture are fashioned
from native chestnut, walnut, oak,
cypress and mountain pine.

water 173

the serene sound of falling water
and its cooling presence in fountains,
ponds, basins and pools are essential
components of the Tuscan garden.

introduction

'Let us look back on Florence while we may, and when its shining dome is seen no more, go travelling through cheerful Tuscany, with a bright remembrance of it; for Italy will be the fairer for the recollection.'

CHARLES DICKENS, *PICTURES FROM ITALY*, (1846)

introduction

When the German poet Goethe toured Tuscany in the 1780s, he was compelled to comment that Tuscany still looked the way Italy ought to look. It seems significant that even then, before industry and automation made their mark on the landscape of Europe, Tuscany stood out as picturesque. Today, more than two centuries on, Goethe's claim retains its resonance. Tuscany, with its postcard views of rustic beauty and Renaissance harmony, is still the quintessential example of pastoral perfection.

What is it about Tuscany that has remained so appealing for centuries? The starting point for the world's love affair with Tuscany is the landscape. It is bordered by the Mediterranean Sea to the west, and by mountains and woodlands to the north and east. Its interior of undulating hills and plains is richly fertile, and a mostly temperate climate makes it idyllic in every sense.

Against a backdrop of natural beauty, the artistic achievements and high culture of Tuscan cities such as Siena, Pisa and Florence seem even more spectacular. After visiting Tuscany in 1844, Charles Dickens wrote of '... the whole sweet valley of the Arno, the convent at Fiesole, the Tower of Galileo, Boccaccio's house, old villas and retreats; innumerable spots of interest, all glowing in a landscape of unsurpassing beauty steeped in the richest light; are spread before us.'

Perhaps, however, it is no coincidence that a region of such 'unsurpassing beauty' has inspired architecture judged to be among the most dazzling of the Renaissance world: the Duomo of Florence; the piazza of Siena; the Leaning Tower of Pisa; and the list goes on. As magnificent as these monuments are, it is the domestic culture of Tuscany that exerts the greater pull on our senses: the food; the crafts; the general texture of daily life; and above all the vernacular architecture. We imagine watching sunsets from a vine-covered stone loggia, tasting tomatoes in a farmhouse kitchen, padding barefoot over cool terracotta floor tiles, or escaping the heat of summer in a garden courtyard. The Tuscan villa – whether a Renaissance villa on a grand scale, or one converted from an old farmhouse – embodies this bucolic ideal.

The great appeal of the Tuscan country home is nothing new. It has been one of the most sought-after living environments for more than a millennium. The original villas of Tuscany were built in ancient times by prominent Romans seeking an escape from the intrigue of politics and from hectic city life. In his letter to Apollinaris, Pliny the Younger writes of his treasured Tuscan villa. He was so taken with it that it became much more than just a summer home. He always described it as his principal seat.

"... let me describe to you the temperateness of the climate, the situation of the country, and the delightfulness of my villa, which will be as agreeable to you to hear as to me to relate ... The greatest part of the house is turn'd to the south, and in the summer from the sixth hour, but in the winter somewhat sooner,

does as it were invite the Sun into a spacious well-proportioned Porticus."

Centuries later, this same description was to inspire the architects of the Renaissance to create villas for the urban aristocracy of the day. As in Roman times, these villas were intended not only to provide physical respite for their owners, but also emotional and intellectual refreshment.

In fifteenth-century Tuscany, the Medici dynasty in particular set the standard for villa construction. Their aim was to create an idealised culture of country life, or *villeggiatura*, as they called it. These were not really places where much in the way of farming work was carried out. Rather, they were places of enjoyment, where the beauties of nature – albeit controlled and contained – could be admired.

Villa architecture then developed over several centuries, and later included the transformation of castles and farmhouses into villas with their own special characteristics. Yet all of these villas share features in common, most especially the materials used in their construction: stone, wood, earth and water. From these four resources come the unique look and sensation of life in Tuscany.

The use of common building materials, all of which are found locally, gives the countryside of Tuscany great visual continuity. The material culture is so distinctive that all except the most modern buildings seem to share common materials and design motifs. Stone walls are the basis for the majority of rural houses, as are terracotta pantiles on the rooftop, terracotta tiles on floors, timber beams and solid wooden doors and shutters. Somewhere too, a water feature will be evident.

Wood is garnered from Tuscany's lush forests of chestnut, beech, white oak and fir. Stone is hewn from the sheer cliffs of the Appenines, inlcuding marble from the quarries at Cararra. The mineral-rich clay that makes Tuscany's renowned terracotta products was deposited in prehistoric times, and later masterfully exploited by the Etruscans. Water is a prominent feature of the landscape – the coast at Maremma and the mountain streams that feed the Rivers Arno and Tiber, among others. It is also an integral component of residential and monastic architecture.

These four elements can be found across the full range of residential period architecture, from farmhouse to villa to palazzo. For example, a stone wash-basin might be the focus of a farmhouse yard, a tinkling fountain – or even a swimming pool – will be present in a villa garden, and a fantastical grotto may lie hidden in the grounds of a palazzo. The application of these materials continues from Roman times in an almost unbroken fashion until the present day. It is this rare sense of continuity – in the look and texture of its buildings above all else – that gives the Tuscan countryside its powerful allure.

stone

'Disposed in several places are marble seats, to ease those that are tired with walking.'

PLINY THE YOUNGER

Set among rolling hills, olive groves, vineyards and chestnut woods, the stone architecture of Tuscany makes an eloquent statement about the region's history and its geology. At the same time, it appeals to the modern eye because of its solidity and authentic patina. Stone is visible almost everywhere in the Tuscan countryside – in lines of rugged farm walls zigzagging across the landscape, in the textured façades of farmhouses and rustic villas, in imposing castles, fortresses and churches, and in the hill towns with their tower houses and remnants of massive ancient walls. These stone structures lend a sense of permanence and continuity to the seasonal changes that are such a part of Tuscan tradition and lifestyle.

Stone has been used from the very earliest times in Tuscany and, while the same can be said of many other parts of Europe, there is something about the character of the region's stone architecture that is especially captivating. The traditional houses of Tuscany fuse the natural beauty of stone with the elegant architectural legacy of the Renaissance and a lively and enduring crafts industry. There are stonemasons and artisans in Tuscany who can provide almost any architectural or decorative detail, true to any historical period, whether medieval, Renaissance or Baroque. However, this enduring culture of stonecraft would arguably not even exist were it not for an abundance of beautiful and durable stone.

Tuscany's particular geology – with hills and mountains of volcanic rock rising steeply from the plains – has provided a wonderful variety of stone that is ideal for building. There are two main types of stone used in Tuscan building: sandstone and limestone. Even within the region, the quality and colour of these stones can vary enormously from province to province. The same is true of marble, which is found in abundance at various sites around Tuscany.

Given these natural resources, it is not surprising that stone plays such a distinctive part in the urban planning, architecture and decoration of Tuscan towns and villages. And anyone building or renovating in the region today cannot help but be overwhelmed by the huge variety of building stone and marble on offer. Sandstone and limestone of varying hues are available, and can be cut and finished in any number of ways. Local marble, too, can be bought in an almost

RIGHT

The terracotta roof tiles of Tuscany are ubiquitous, creating a sense of architectural unity in towns and villages across the region. The Etruscans were the first to use terracotta roof tiles in Tuscany, although the Romans developed the style of laying tiles largely used today.

Since the fifteenth century when quarrying began in earnest, Tuscan builders and architects have had access to a fantastic range of good building stone, from white Carrara marble to limestone and sandstone.

infinite variety of colourings. Its aesthetic appeal and its durability make it an enormously versatile material for all kinds of exterior detailing and interior finishes, something that the Romans recognised and exploited across their empire.

The marble of the Apuan Alps has been quarried for around two thousand years. Running across the northern border of Tuscany, on the western coast between Pisa and La Spezia, the Apuan Alps (or *Alpi Apuane* as they are called in Italian) are a branch of the Apennines. These mountains are a limestone formation, and have provided generations of builders with limestone blocks, as well as the famed marble that is quarried at Carrara, Seravezza, Massa and Pietrasanta.

The Romans were among the first to use and exploit the characteristic white, dove-grey and streaky grey-and-white marbles of this area. Following in their footsteps, the architects and sculptors of the Renaissance prized the marble of Carrara and used it widely. As with so many other Renaissance trends, the use of marble filtered down to all but the humblest homes. Whether in the form of a palazzo ('palace') façade, a fountain in a villa garden or a simple basin in the kitchen, the 'white gold' of Carrara has become a staple element of Tuscan living.

Despite the high reputation of Carrara marble since Roman times, and perhaps because of its expense, Tuscan builders and sculptors have traditionally sourced marble from all over the region. In contrast to the luminescent white Carrara marble, there are several types of highly coloured marble found near the banks of the Arno. These include: *tigrato* – yellow with black specks; *pilora di Arno* – greenish yellow with pink and black specks; and the sought-after *garatonio*, which has a red background flecked with golden veins.

Monte Arrenti is known for its very hard, green- and violet-hued marble, while yellow marbles are quarried at Marmoraja. There are black marbles from Barga and grey marbles from Grassino and Siena. Also from Siena and at nearby Montarenti are rich yellow marble varieties, some with delicate blue-red and purple veins, others with a reddish tint.

While white Carrara marble has remained the stone of choice for sculptors over the centuries, the coloured marbles of Tuscany have found equal favour among architects and furniture-makers. The Medicis were particularly fond of coloured marbles, especially new and unusual varieties. Some of their favourite marble came from Seravezza, not far from Carrara in the Apuan Alps. *Mischio di Seravezza* is a deep violet colour with clouds of pink, and shortly after it was discovered in the late sixteenth century it was used by the Medici grand dukes for some of their Florentine monuments – in the Neptune fountain of the Piazza della Signoria, for example. A related stone is *Breccia di Seravezza*, which features fragments of white, pink and green set against a background of deep violet. In later centuries this prized marble was often incorporated into furnishings, for the tops of console tables and commodes – a fashion that continues to this day.

The variety of building stone in Tuscany is equally impressive in its range and quality. Perhaps the most revered of the Tuscan stones is sandstone, extensive deposits of which are found on the southern slopes of the Apennines. Quarries have been worked for centuries on the hillsides above Fiesole and Settignano, especially at Monte Céceri.

Pietra serena and *pietra bigia* are both fine-grained sandstones from Fiesole, prized for their texture. *Pietra serena* is pale, while *pietra bigia* is a darker version of the stone. They were used together to great effect by Michelangelo in the Biblioteca Laurenziana at the church of San Lorenzo in Florence, where great columns, balustrades and stairs were wrought in the dark stone, and contrasted with the stark white plaster. The fine grain of this stone meant that it could be carved with elaborate detail, and today there are several varieties of this grey sandstone available to architects and builders.

The *pietra serena* widely used in Renaissance times, and seen all around Florence, is still one of the favourite building stones of Tuscan architects. Tightly grained and a uniform medium-grey, it is easy to work and combines well with other materials such as marble and wood. It is used both for interiors and exteriors and will withstand the demands of cold as well as warm climates.

Another classic grey sandstone is *pietra medicea*, used for centuries as cobblestones, for paving, cubic stonework and wall cladding. These days it is often used for flooring, window surrounds and sills, fireplaces and furniture. The elegant *pietra forte colombino* is one of the hardest of sandstones. With a beautifully fine texture and dark-grey colouring, it is typically used for the most exclusive projects.

While the grey varieties are the best-known Tuscan sandstones, there are also types of quartz sandstone with different colour tones. Quartz sandstone in subtle shades of deep red, as well as creamy yellow, is quarried near Florence, and is used not only for exterior cladding and detailing but also for interiors and paving.

Tuscany has long proved a rich source of limestone, which is now exported around the world. In medieval and Renaissance times, building stone was dug up from the banks of the Arno, all the way along the river between Santa Margherita a Montici and Monte Oliveto. Limestone blocks are known to have been extensively quarried by the Romans, and probably by the Etruscans before that. The great advantage of limestone is that it can be hewn into huge blocks, which makes it ideal for walls and solid masonry. Dressed limestone – cut in a square or rectangular shape, and presenting a smooth or decorated surface – has been extensively used in Tuscany for centuries.

The hills around Florence offer access to excellent supplies of good limestone – *pietra forte*. This distinctive sandy-brown limestone has been used widely for building since medieval times, and probably even earlier. The demand in Renaissance times was so great that there were even quarries in the city

RIGHT

Framed by towering cypress trees, stands the quintessential stone farmhouse of Tuscany, comprising a tower – possibly dating back to medieval times – with various rooms added on over the years.

RIGHT

Historically, rural houses were built from whatever materials lay

closest to hand. Often, this meant the rough fieldstone that sat close

to the surface of the soil, a legacy of Tuscany's volcanic topography.

of Florence, minimizing transport time and costs. Up until the sixteenth century there was a major quarry at the Santa Felicità convent, now the Boboli Gardens. Florentine stonemasons have become renowned for their craft of refining the local limestone into articulated blocks and ornamental elements.

Dressed limestone or sandstone was used mainly for civic and religious buildings and major residential architecture. It was used only sparingly for country houses, incorporated with undressed stone. This can be seen all over Tuscany today. Only substantial and luxurious villas present a façade entirely of dressed stone.

The most common type of stone is that found naturally in the landscape – usually rough, undressed limestone. Essentially fieldstone, these loose blocks have (over time) become separated from ledges by natural processes and scattered on the ground. A readily available material for building, this stone has always been at hand for constructing walls, towers, farmhouses and villas in the countryside. This is the stone that gives the Tuscan landscape its essential character, and from the earliest days was used for foundations and fortifications.

The Etruscans were quick to recognise the properties of Tuscan stone. Although they built mainly with wood, they drew on stone for the foundations of their houses and temples, for their tombs, and for fortifications on the hilltop sites where they established their towns. Vestiges of their building skills can still be found in the Tuscan hill towns. Volterra has Etruscan walls, a city gate and sixth-century BC tombs all of stone, and even an ancient mine for alabaster, from which they carved urns and vessels.

The city walls at Cortona date from this time. Henry James described encountering the massive stone blocks of the hill town's Etruscan walls:

'In the afternoon I came down and hustled a while through the crowded little streets, and then strolled forth under the scorching sun and made the outer circuit of the wall. There I found tremendous uncemented blocks; they glared and twinkled in the powerful light, and I had to put on a blue eye-glass in order to throw into its proper perspective the vague Etruscan past, obtruded and magnified in such masses quite as with the effect of inadequately withdrawn hands and feet in photographs.'

Following in Etruscan footsteps, the Romans were well aware of the importance of building for posterity (having razed the Etruscans' wooden wellings). They established a building tradition that used stone and marble, and quarried limestone and marble from the Apuan Alps. They developed a highly sophisticated means of mass production, quarrying vast quantities of marble from their colony at Luni (north of Pisa and below present-day Carrara). The Romans were also the first to exploit Carrara for marble.

There is no exact date for when quarrying began, but certainly by around 40 BC the Romans had begun to extract the local marble. The Carrione River, with its source at Carrara, ran down to the sea close to Luni, and it was probably during their forays upstream that the Romans discovered deposits of white and grey Carrara marble. Once the quarries at Luni were established, about 12 km (8 miles) from the city, an efficient production line was set up. First the blocks were separated with trenches, then broken away with pickaxes, chisels and wedges. Often the roughly cut blocks were shipped throughout the Mediterranean and northern Europe for cutting and carving at their final destination, but there was also a lively industry in ready-made marble sculptures, columns and architectural details. Carrara became one of the major quarries of Imperial Rome. Marble was loaded on to carts and transported by road to Luni, then shipped out of Luni harbour.

Luni continued to supply huge amounts of Carrara marble until the eventual decline of the Roman Empire. The last recorded monument of the era to be built from Carrara marble was the Foca column at the Forum, erected around 608. By that time Luni had become little more than a ghost town, but so much marble had been extracted during the Roman era that there was plenty around for the locals to recycle. Right through to the Middle Ages, Roman sites in Tuscany (as elsewhere in Italy) were frequently plundered for building material, especially the prized white marble.

Between the fall of the Roman Empire and the early Middle Ages there was minimal demand for new building materials. Btween the fourth and tenth centuries was a period of great disruption and destruction: warring factions within Tuscany routinely raided each other's towns, and there was little opportunity for expansion.

All this changed, however, from the twelfth century, when trade routes opened to the East as a result of the First Crusades. Pisa was quick to establish trading links, and Siena and Florence also became major players in trade as well as the first banking cities. Wealth began to accumulate, and for the first time in centuries there was the impetus to begin building on a major scale. The first need was for security, as competition among rival cities was fierce. The Florentines, for example, tore down every civic building in neighbouring Fiesole. It was war of the bitterest kind. In this state of constant flux, where the fabric of a city might be destroyed more or less overnight if it fell prey to a rival, it is not surprising that city rulers emphasised solid, impenetrable structures – and what better material for this than stone.

Most critically, stone was used to build defensive walls. A strong and solid wall, encircling and enclosing the land, the buildings and the people, became the most important requirement of the medieval Tuscan city. It had gates that were guarded by day and secured against invasion by night. It had towers for lookout posts, and emplacements for soldiers to fight from, if necessary. In short, the defensive stone wall was the defining characteristic of the city. Not only did the wall dictate the city's safety; it also helped to shape the way in which the town developed and how it was planned.

Transportation of stone – particularly the amounts required for enormous fortified walls – was a key issue for medieval planners. The increasing demand for stone and marble forced them to act, building roads to facilitate increased quantities of stone being moved from quarry to city. New roads were built along the valley floor, rather than along the hilltop ridges as they had been before, and they were paved in order to withstand the heavy cargoes of stone across the countryside.

Beyond the major Tuscan cities – on the plains, and in the hill towns above – the idea of defensive architecture also took root, influencing the style of domestic building. The typical country house of the landowner was a stone tower built from undressed, rough-hewn limestone. It was modelled along the lines of tower houses in the cities and towns, but it was designed to offer protection as a priority. It had a few small windows and little decoration, other than perhaps castellations. Square in plan, it had a single room per floor, connected by a staircase.

In those days, the countryside was a dangerous place. The reality was that most rural folk, including those peasants that worked on the land, lived within the safe confines of the walled hill towns, or inside the walls of fortressed villages or the walled castle of a landowner. They ventured out to the fields to work during the day, but returned before nightfall.

Within the walls of hill towns such as Poppi, rows of low stone houses were built to house cattle and other livestock at street level, with a room or two above for the workers. Architecture was purely functional.

While there are some other medieval influences still apparent in the interiors of rural Tuscan houses – such as the technique of multicoloured marble cladding and inlay that continues from the late medieval Romanesque architectural style – most domestic architecture visible today is more reflective of the Renaissance. This period of intellectual and artistic brilliance, between the fourteenth and sixteenth centuries, dramatically changed the look of the Tuscan cities. Rural architecture benefited from these developments, too. Up until then, farmhouses and tower houses were typically made from rubble or fieldstone. Sometimes they might even have incorporated elements scavenged from a local Roman ruin. During the Renaissance, however, aesthetic concerns increasingly dominated urban and pastoral architecture, and both the application of stone and the types of stone available became more refined.

The origins of Renaissance architecture lie in the Tuscan city-states of Florence, Lucca, Pisa and Siena, which embarked on major building programmes to cater for the growth in population, and to reflect their wealth and status. New cathedrals, churches and public buildings were required, along with paved streets and fountains, and the tax revenue

OPPOSITE

The hill towns of Tuscany are built almost entirely from stone, reflecting their role as safe havens. During the troubled Middle Ages, when the open countryside was a dangerous place after nightfall, the hilltowns with their impenetrable, fortress-like walls offered protection.

generated by the more populous cities gave local governments more to spend on civic works. Similarly, in the private sphere, wealth acquired from the businesses of banking or trade, particularly in Florence and Siena, was used to build new family palaces or remodel existing ones.

This time it was not just functional building stone that was required for construction. Aesthetics increasingly became an important consideration. Civic governments in Tuscany instituted a strictly regulated code to ensure that any new works enhanced the appearance of the city. In Siena, one provision of the fourteenth century declared:

'Because it redounds to the beauty of the city of Siena ... that any edifices that are to be made anew ... proceed in line with the existing buildings, and one building should not stand out beyond another, but they shall be disposed and arranged equally so as to be of greatest beauty for the city.'

These sentiments were embraced by the other Tuscan city-states; indeed, competition was fierce between them, and each city was desperate to outdo its rivals in the splendour of its buildings. One of the most effective and impressive ways of enhancing any building or public space was through sculpture and statuary. The quality and quantity of such adornments came to be seen as an indicator of a city's wealth and, as a symbol of urban success, elaborate sculptural decoration on a grand scale was highly effective. As the well-worn tourist trail through Tuscan cities still attests, a magnificently decorated

cathedral façade or a splendid fountain embellished with sculptures makes an immediate impression on any visitor. In fourteenth-century Tuscany, therefore, there was a huge demand for statuary materials. The finest of all materials for sculpture was marble, and the finest marble came from Carrara.

With improved methods of transportation, more types of marble were quarried and made available to architects and sculptors around Tuscany. With its particular qualities for surface decoration, it was the natural material of choice for building and decorating the fine monuments and structures of the rich Tuscan city-states. Marble was also mastered to sensational effect by the most celebrated sculptors of the age – Nicola Pisano, Arnolfo di Cambio and Andrea Pisano were among the famed marble-carvers who were commissioned by cities and wealthy private patrons. To own and display such marble carving was the ultimate symbol of wealth and power.

As the Renaissance unfolded, new styles of architecture evolved to express the intellectual and aesthetic changes in taste. To meet the new structural and decorative demands of the new buildings, architects turned to *pietra serena*. This soft grey sandstone had been used before the Renaissance, but from the fifteenth century it came into its own. It was used so extensively that it became synonymous with Florence, and with the Italian Renaissance in general. The appeal was understandable: it was fine-grained and therefore good for rendering ornamental detail. It was also relatively inexpensive.

RIGHT

Bathed in afternoon sunlight, a simple farmhouse, or casa colonica, makes an idyllic emblem of pastoral life. The casa colonica often evolved from a tower (the tallest section at the far end of this house) with one room per floor. In medieval times, the tower provided an essential defence for isolated country dwellers.

Of course people in Tuscany had used this type of building stone in a rough, unarticulated fashion for many years. The landowners in the hills around Florence had hardly bothered to exploit the deposits of stone by setting up quarries because the stone was so widespread. In the past, when a builder needed the stone, he would agree a price with the landowner, then simply extract the stone himself and take it away. Now, through the formal architecture of the Renaissance, *pietra serena* was very much in demand. Quarries needed to supply a steady stream of the stone for all the new building works in Florence, as well as for the elegant new villas that began springing up all around Tuscany.

As the countryside became more civilised during the relative peace of the Renaissance, some of the landowners still living in stone tower houses adapted and added to the structures, to make more expansive, comfortable homes. Sometimes landowners added rooms at the base of the tower, and the tower itself became the dovecote – doves and pigeons were kept as much for consumption by the inhabitants as for killing pests, eating weeds and providing manure.

Many landowners abandoned the old tower houses in order to build anew, however, and often gave them to the farmers on their estates (during the Renaissance, farmers had started to move out of the hill towns and on to the land). If they were not lucky enough to have inherited a tower house, farmers lived in a simple one- or two-roomed house, shared by the animals. As the farmhouse was supplied by the landowner, there was usually no room for architectural refinement – its structure and style (a simple rough stone dwelling built from fieldstone) reflected the fact that it was the house of a working farm.

But gradually things changed. The overhaul of the medieval feudal system enabled peasant farmers to share in the profits of the estate. As the farmers became more prosperous, they added more refined features – quoins (external corners of walls) of cut stone, loggias, porticos, and windows framed in cut stone – all reflecting the style of their well-to-do neighbours. This was the beginning of the *casa colonica*, the characteristic Tuscan farmhouse.

The aristocratic landowners who had once only visited their estates from time to time now saw the country life as an attractive alternative to the bustling city. Just as the ancient Roman scholar, Pliny, had built a villa in Tuscany, the wealthy Italians of the Renaissance period also longed for a country retreat in the Classical style. This was not only a base for overseeing their land, but a place for intellectual contemplation and appreciation of aesthetic concerns. The new country homes of the nobility reflected this, often using the same building materials and decorative devices as their palazzi in town: dressed sandstone or limestone for the façade, and marble tiles for the floors, marble-clad stairs, windowsills and other architectural elements.

Also colonizing the countryside was a new breed of rural dweller – prosperous bankers and merchants who sought rest from their hectic urban lives. They bought a parcel of farmland with a small house where the family could retreat for the long hot summers – just as the middle classes of Italy do nowadays. In some cases these newcomers would commission a new villa from scratch; in other cases the existing house on the land might be extended and renovated.

A medieval castle could be transformed into an imposing and luxurious residence; an ancient stone tower house could form the centrepiece of a new building; or an old farmhouse could be expanded into a small villa incorporating elegant Renaissance features. This became known as a *villa-fattoria* (literally 'country house-farm').

Like the grander villas of the landed nobility, the *villa-fattoria* featured a stone loggia, a portico, and the Classical proportions of a Renaissance floor-plan. Floors were made of cut limestone, sandstone or terracotta, often with patterns inlaid. Windows and doors were symmetrically arranged and framed in cut stone. The garden was enhanced with stone and marble fountains and statuary.

By the end of the Renaissance, the vogue for stone façades was fading, particularly among the wealthy. The new fashion was for stuccoed and plastered façades. Although stone still played a part in the decoration and ornamentation of villas, it now tended to be a secondary one. Stone and marble were still used most notably in the garden, though. This was the age of artifice in nature. Pebble-mosaiced walkways, stone or marble fountains, grottoes made of pumice or tufa and set with seashells, statues and colonnades – all were important elements of the sixteenth-century Mannerist garden, and are still very much evident in the grand villas of Tuscany.

It was not until the eigtheenth century, when Tuscany was 'rediscovered' by European artists and intellectuals, that the medieval and Renaissance character of the Tuscan villa became fashionable again. Tuscany and its way of living seemed to embody the Romantic ideals of the time. The Romantic obsession with antiquity and nature was well met in the golden light, the picturesque views and the hill towns seemingly untouched by modernity.

Even today, the Tuscan villa is viewed as the quintessential retreat, and the stone walls and façades are much admired for their aesthetic appeal. Restoration or renovation of a Tuscan house inevitably focuses on retaining and reinstating the massive stone walls that have probably remained since medieval or Renaissance times. Now, as centuries ago, villa owners prize the texture and integrity of unadorned stone.

Looking at the rural dwellings of modern-day Tuscany, it is not difficult to see the enduring legacy of stone architecture from ancient times through to the Renaissance. The façades of many farmhouses and small villas reveal a layering of historical periods. Exterior walls are typically composed of

rubble or rough fieldstone, and they are easy to spot. The stones are relatively small and uneven, and their texture is rough and weathered. But this rough stonework will likely have been modified over the years to take on an altogether more elegant and Classical appearance.

All but the humblest farmhouse has window frames of dressed stone, usually limestone but possibly even fine grey *pietra serena*. The same dressed stone is used to delineate the arch around a doorway, or for the arches of a loggia or portico.

The loggia is in essence an arcaded gallery that runs along one side of the house or wraps around it. A loggia may be open on one or more sides, providing an airy, shaded place for relaxation or outdoor eating, and marking the transition to the garden. In many Tuscan villas, the loggia features vaulted ceilings and carved stone corbels. The arches will be edged with a border of dressed stone, or possibly trimmed with terracotta bricks. The loggia might also include marble or stone benches as seating.

The portico is also a roofed space, and is either open or enclosed, but tends to be smaller than the loggia. It is a design feature of the front of the house, forming the entrance and centrepiece of the stone façade. A Tuscan portico often

incorporates graceful stone or marble columns; above it, the various storeys of the villa may be defined by stone cornices.

The stone façades of the larger and more luxurious villas, particularly those built for wealthy landowners in Renaissance times, make greater use of cut stone. These blocks of rectangular stone tend to be large and evenly sized, and often have a smooth or articulated surface. This is quarried stone which has been cut and finished, or 'dressed'.

Elaborate dressed stone is often used for the window and door surrounds of villas. This type of stone features patterns cut into it to create decorative detail. The tradition of decorated stone for architectural elements dates from the late Renaissance, when it became fashionable for stone to exhibit the grooves of the stonemason's claw chisel. The pale-grey *pietra serena* sandstone is used in abundance in this fashion on the façades of the larger country villas.

Universally applied to almost all Tuscan architecture is the use of dressed stone for quoins – the stones at the corner of a wall that look quite distinct by their size, projection, rustication, or by a different finish. Even the roughest of stone walls in Tuscany seems to feature a large rectangular quoin. They lend a sense of refinement to stone architecture, and are

ABOVE

In numerous Tuscan hill towns, cobbled lanes wind past alleys of terraced houses and under the arches of ancient walls. Built from massive blocks of stone, these walls were a crucial fortification in the Middle Ages.

OPPOSITE

The style of this terrace of worker's houses, or casette a schiera, dates back at least to medieval times. The wide door at street level would once have served as the entrance to a workshop, with rooms for living arranged above.

a key device in setting apart primitive stone structures from those that are more architecturally complex.

The traditional stone flooring of Tuscany is likewise a study in the masterful application of raw materials. Among Tuscan farmhouses and villas, there is a superb array of finishes and designs through which decorative taste can be expressed. In the simplest, most rustic form, floors are simple stone slabs of cut (but undressed) limestone or sandstone. For exterior areas, they can take the form of natural cobblestones. Parquetry is another option, with stone floors inlaid in patterns consisting of two or more colours or materials.

At its most decorative, flooring in Tuscany employs marble; terrazzo is one example of marble surfacing and has been in use since Roman times. It is a type of concrete in which chips or pieces of stone (usually marble) are mixed with cement and ground to a flat surface, thus exposing the chips which take a high polish. More elaborate than terrazzo is marble inlay for flooring, with the marble supplied as a slab or in the form of large tiles.

The use of marble inlay and the combining of multicoloured marbles for decorative purposes has its history in the architecture of the late Middle Ages. At this time, a uniquely Tuscan style of Romanesque architecture developed. Most private dwellings and many civic and religious buildings of the age were constructed from rubble and brick but with a cladding of stone or marble, presenting a more impressive façade.

Tuscan Romanesque architecture shared many of the same formal criteria as Romanesque architecture in other parts of Europe. The shape of arches, vaulting and layouts were commonly derived from Classical Roman architecture, but – uniquely in Tuscany and some other parts of Italy – marble cladding was used as surface decoration, often using several colours and featuring intricate inlay.

The Tuscan Romanesque style was all about surface appearance, and this idea is still very much in evidence in the region's villas and farmhouses – not so much for the exterior, but for interior detailing. As marble has been used for centuries, it is employed for fireplaces, flooring, staircases and windowsills (among other applications), and plays an important aesthetic role when incorporated into furnishings. A slab of particularly striking marble makes a distinctive and hard-wearing table-top. Its durability also makes marble well suited for the carving of sinks and bowls, or for statues, fountains and furniture for the garden. There are few more evocative elements in the Tuscan villa than a simple marble fountain or bench.

Whether the white- or grey-streaked marbles of Carrara, or any of the highly coloured Tuscan marbles; whether creamy-yellow limestone or fine grey sandstone, the natural stone of Tuscany imbues the local architecture with a sense of artless beauty. Now, just as in the days of Pliny, stone is used in subtle yet elegant ways, elevating the simplest farmhouse into a refined country residence.

OPPOSITE

A villa façade combines elements of rusticity and refinement in a typically Tuscan manner. The rough stone retaining wall below constrasts with the smooth stuccoed walls of the house above. An architrave of grey stone adds definition.

BELOW

The proportions and sloping angle of this massive wall indicate the base of a tower or fortification. Its stuccoed rendering is worn in places to reveal grey stone underneath.

RIGHT

No Tuscan villa is complete without a loggia, providing a protected and private place for eating al fresco, or simply for admiring the view of the countryside. It is usually open on one or more sides to catch cooling breezes, with a roof to give shelter from the sun. This picturesque loggia is set on a stone floor, under a canopy of vines on a wooden trellis.

ABOVE

An ancient stone reservoir surrounded by wildflowers makes a charming water feature in a wild Tuscan garden, where chickens are free to roam.

LEFT

The brick edging around this wide arched doorway brings a sense of symmetry to the arrangement of buildings around the courtyard. The double row of bricks is a traditional decorative device for embellishing stone and stucco façades.

OPPOSITE

The laying of stone for decorative purposes, particularly in mosaic form, was developed by the ancient Romans. Renaissance gardeners perpetuated the passion for patterned stonework with their intricate, pebble-set pavements.

ABOVE

Tuscan architecture through the ages has demonstrated an imaginative and ingenious range of treatments for doorways. In Renaissance times the doorway was given special attention, as its placement was key to establishing the symmetry and harmony of a building façade. Treatments include edging in stone blocks to blend with the wall; edging with brick or in contrasting stone; stone lintels and pediment; and edging with raised stone blocks.

LEFT & ABOVE

A superb feat of stone engineering, this tunnel vault runs the length of the villa exterior to create a shady arched terrace for dining. The vaulting springs from massive rectangular stone pillars, indicating that the origins of the building may have been a fortress or monastery.

RIGHT

The linear proportions of a stone façade and a courtyard paved with flagstones are balanced by the curves of the doorway and window.

OPPOSITE

A profusion of vines laden with pink blooms, together with tubs and vases over-flowing with flowers, softens the bare stone walls and scrubbed wooden furniture of a sunny courtyard.

ABOVE

The light fittings in an interior designer's Tuscan home have been cleverly fashioned to mimic the stone wall behind.

RIGHT

Interior stone walls are typically covered in stucco and sometimes coated with whitewash – here the rough textures and protruding shapes of the stones lend a rugged feel to a farmhouse entrance.

OPPOSITE

Large, irregular slabs of travertine make a striking feature in the living area of a renovated villa. The subtle bands of colour in the stone and its relatively fine grain make travertine beautifully suited to polishing.

OPPOSITE & ABOVE

An unusual Tuscan residence mixes medieval austerity with luxurious touches. The magnificent walls are kept

bare to show off the texture and colour of the different stones and to contrast with the furnishings. Plush

crimson upholstery, a deep leather armchair, large rugs in tawny shades and a beautiful chandelier bring warmth

to thc bare stone walls. The end result is a mood of baronial splendour, conjured with a light touch.

OPPOSITE

Even a simple stone staircase takes on a light and elegant appearance with the addition of a decorative balustrade in wrought iron – a traditional Tuscan craft.

ABOVE & RIGHT

Ornamental detail is a key part of any Tuscan interior scheme. The balustrade can providethe means for bringing visual interest to an austere backdrop of white washed walls.

BELOW

The use of marble for table and console tops has been fashionable in Tuscany for centuries. Here, the edges have been expertly sculpted to create an elegant piece that serves as a sideboard.

LEFT

An open staircase with a carved stone balustrade is framed by a matching pair of columns with Ionic capitals. This dramatic vestibule, designed in neo-gothic style, was built in the mid-nineteenth century during the renovation of the medieval Castello Brolio, on the renowned wine-growing estate in Chianti.

BELOW

Stone decoration comes into its own in the Tuscan garden – whether in the form of organic carving around a window, in the wave-like scroll on the border of a path or in the crenellation and crest of a stone basin.

OPPOSITE

A sweeping stone stairway leads to the portico of a villa façade. Although the exterior has weathered over the years, the scale of the entrance and the detail evident in the stone finials and mouldings indicate grand origins.

ABOVE

The tradition of sculpture in stone and marble lives on in Tuscany in numerous workshops and quarries. The Renaissance sculptors of Florence were renowned for their skill in transforming marble into great works of art, and they took the task of choosing marble very carefully. The very best, and most expensive material for sculpture was the snowy-white marble of Carrara. Michelangelo was known to travel to the quarries there to personally choose marble blocks for each commission, including that of the statue David.

LEFT

The grounds at Villa Torrigiani are one of the few remaining examples of seventeenth-century Tuscan landscaping and garden design. As was characteristic of the period, water and stone were the dominant elements. Stone was used for constructing everything from staircases and statues to fountains, grottoes and garden seating.

RIGHT

The inhabitants of Tuscan towns have long been known for their civic pride, reflected in even the most mundane public object. Here, a fixture for tethering horses, attached to a stone wall, is a miniature work of art.

BELOW

The stone basin is one of the most enduring garden features. Used since ancient times as a place for washing and drinking, it now serves more as ornament in almost every Tuscan outdoor space, from courtyard to formal garden. This basin bears the mark of the mason's chisel.

RIGHT

A stone arch and pathway set with stone provide the backdrop for a pretty walkway. A trellis constructed overhead and laden with vines offers shade.

Layers of stone are revealed in this garden staircase. Rough-textured tufa makes up the underlying wall, with rectangular stone slabs aligned on top to support the triangular-shaped risers and treads. Carved balustrades complete the structure.

RIGHT

Animal heads and grotesque masks were common architectural motifs in Tuscany during the Mannerist age of the sixteenth century, and often appeared in the form of a fountain with a stream of water issuing from the mouth.

OPPOSITE

An outdoor stairway of stone, set with a wrought-iron balustrade, is softened with a wash of pale pink on the adjoining walls and a profusion of bright geraniums.

wood

'Baccio d'Agnolo again took chisel in hand, and blocks of dark walnut wood were transformed by magic into the most exquisite furniture.'

SCOTT LEADER, *TUSCAN STUDIES AND SKETCHES* (1888)

There is one element in Tuscan architecture and decoration that is more connected to the landscape than any other. Wood is the organic material that subtly relates the villa to its surroundings. More evocative than stone, stronger and more elemental than terracotta, wood creates a powerful visual link between the man-made structure of the house and the countryside beyond. When used unpainted, simply varnished or polished to highlight the patina, wood is a charming and beautiful component of the Tuscan house. Indeed, wood adds a necessary warmth and texture to even the most humble stone *casa colonica*, or farmhouse.

Wood is the classic substance of rustic construction and furnishing. Its solidity is comforting, and it is smooth and welcoming to the touch. Visually, it needs no surface decoration – the natural grain of the wood is beautiful enough. Whether used in its basic state, inlaid, carved or painted, or used indoors or outdoors, wood creates an intimate link between the built environment of the farmhouse or villa and the classic landscape of central Italy.

An enduring characteristic of pastoral Tuscany is the close relationship between the people and their surroundings. They like to put their mark upon the land and tame it, and over the centuries they have artfully shaped the countryside to create the picturesque scenes we are so familiar with today. Judiciously using natural elements to fashion a controlled, idealised rural enclaves, the Tuscans have made the land more livable and ultimately highly pleasing to the eye. To do this, they have used trees, the most malleable and transplantable of natural resources.

Trees, therefore, define the landscape of Tuscany; in both spontaneous and contrived ways, they have become the most distinctive natural features of the countryside. Wild woods are scattered across the region, many of which have been pared back from their original size but nevertheless remain intact as forest ecosystems. By far the most prominent clusters of trees in the landscape are there by human intervention. There are trees planted for agriculture – olive trees, almond trees, walnut trees, lemon, orange and other fruit trees, as well as the supple branches of grape vines. Trees are also arranged as a way of marking and carving up the fabric of the countryside. Tall cypresses line driveways and cluster around villages, cutting a line across

RIGHT

Tuscany has been renowned through the ages for its well-stocked forests, making wood a ready and abundant resource. It has been used to make nearly every com-modity of material life, from carved Etruscan temples and Renaissance furniture suites to the humble farmer's cart.

the hills where a road winds up and over, or acting as a windbreak at the edge of farming land or as a privacy screen surrounding a villa or providing shade beside a pool.

Such quintessentially Tuscan scenes have been admired over the centuries. Writing of the gardens at the Medici villa at Castello in 1580, Michel de Montaigne described several gardens as 'admirably laid out, all of them on the slope of a hill so that all the straight walks are upon a descent, but a very gentle and easy one; the cross walks are level and terraced. In every direction you see a variety of arbours, thickly formed of every description of odiferous trees, cedars, cypresses, orange trees, lemon trees, and olive trees, the branches of which are so closely interwoven that the sun, at its meridian height, cannot penetrate them.'

Paintings of the era, such as Benozzo Gozzoli's *Procession of the Magi* (1459), show idyllic rural scenes in which trees are the dominant points of reference. Bearing fruit and planted in rows, trees signify the orchards on which the country villa relies for fresh fruit. Growing either side of roads and lanes, they mark the route that lies ahead of the traveller. And, huddled in thick clusters of the same arboreal family, they indicate plantations for wood. As Gozzoli's painting so richly conveys, Tuscany is blessed with trees in abundance – and not just any trees. They are some of the very finest trees yielding hardwood for building and furniture-making.

For centuries, Tuscan carpenters and artisans have enjoyed the best selection of wood in Italy. Whether Etruscan builders, Renaissance architects or the talented creators of lavish Baroque furniture, all drew on the beautiful forests of the region. As recently as 1832, one third of the land in the region was estimated to be covered in forest, and today Tuscany still has more woodland than anywhere else in Italy. From the coast with its pine woods to the mountains stocked with alpine species, there is an astounding variety of trees.

Along coastal areas of Tuscany, aromatic Mediterranean shrubs thrive alongside vast holly and pine woods. The Maremma on the south coast is especially rich in vegetation, with pines, evergreen oaks and towering cork trees providing majestic scenery. Further inland there are forests of white oak, and the chestnut woods and groves for which the region is famous. At remote San Galgano, surrounded by dense woodlands, the monks of the abbey became wealthy selling the trees for fuel and building timber. In Abetone and Vallombrosa, to the east of Florence, there are ancient forests of tall firs, oak, chestnut and beech trees. Higher up, along the border with Emilia-Romagna, the Casentinesi Forests provide the ideal terrain and high humidity for growth of ancient silver firs, beeches, maples, aspen, oak, lime and elm. Below the alpine pastures of the Apennines, mountain forests of beech and fir grow in abundance and, in the far north of Tuscany, between the Orecchiella Mountains and the Apuane Alps, are the verdant wooded valleys and alpine tree species of the Garfagnana region.

Much of Tuscany's woodland comprises coppices of low trees, which have been felled and regenerated over the course of centuries to supply timber for fuel. Certain wooded areas – fir and chestnut forests in particular – provide timber for building. Other Tuscan trees ideal for building with are oaks, beeches, larches and pines. Their strength makes them highly suited to load-bearing construction. These resources are strictly controlled, to ensure a sustainable supply for the future.

In ancient times, before the land had been cleared and 'civilised', forests covered the landscape. In his book *Etruscan Places*, D. H. Lawrence mused that:

'In Etruscan days ... the pleasant pineta, or open, sparse forest of umbrella pines, once spread on and on, with tall arbutus and heather covering the earth from which the reddish trunks rose ...'

It is no wonder, then, that the Etruscans chose to build from wood. The region they inhabited, named Tuscany after them, was so densely covered with trees yielding soft and hard woods that they were the most obvious and most accessible building material. Houses could be erected quickly, and without the hard labour required to excavate and haul stone. The Etruscans also loved surface decoration and wood was superbly malleable for engraving or carving.

Lawrence lamented that so little of the Etruscan civilisation remained. There are stone tombs, carved into hillsides across central Italy, which he visited and described in great detail, and there are artefacts (mostly urns, vases and vessels) attesting to the Etruscans' pottery-making skills. But the most significant material element of their civilisation has disappeared – their wooden buildings. As Lawrence explained, 'the Etruscans built everything of wood – houses, temples – all save walls of fortification, great gates, bridges and drainage works. So that the Etruscan cities vanished as completely as flowers.'

Unlike the empire-building Romans (who constructed from stone), the carefree Etruscans lived for the moment, and little of their legacy remains in terms of wooden construction. Perhaps their most enduring contribution to the vernacular architecture of Tuscany is in the Tuscan column style. This perfectly simple, smoothly curved column has been used in the façades and terraces of houses throughout the region for more than five hundred years.

Although now wrought in stone, marble or plaster, the Tuscan column was originally made from wood. In 1562, Giacomo Barozzi da Vignola set out the five orders of columns to be used in architecture – specifying their characteristics and proportions – which are still the accepted standards today. In his book, *Manual for the Five Orders of Architecture*, Vignola admires the Tuscan Order for its simplicity, plain appearance and bulk. It was made from the fewest number of parts and

was considered capable of bearing very heavy loads. The Tuscan column is thought to have derived from the wooden ones used in Etruscan buildings, which would explain its plain appearance, for unlike other types of Classical column it bore no fluting or other decorative flourishes. It was considered most

suitable for utilitarian constructions such as farm buildings, and even the distance between two Tuscan columns was wide enough for a horse-drawn wagon or cart to fit through.

Apart from the Tuscan column's origins, the wooden construction of the Etruscans has long since been forgotten. From the Roman period onwards, building switched to stone or brick. Wood was relegated to a secondary role in architecture, used primarily as lumber for certain structural elements. In the guild records of the Renaissance, when building activity in Tuscany was at a peak, wood does not feature as an important building material. Its main uses were for scaffolding, and for ceiling spaces that needed to be spanned by wooden beams. By far the most widespread use of wood (apart from providing fuel) was for making furniture.

This is also fairly true for modern times, for the Tuscan houses visible across the landscape today, many of which are centuries old, are built predominantly out of stone. Very little timber is visible from the outside – usually only the front door and window shutters. Rather, timber is reserved for the interior – for beams, roof supports, internal doors and furniture.

Without doubt the most prominent wooden feature of Tuscan construction is the ceiling. This is almost universally the case, regardless of building style – a ceiling can comprise rugged beams in a rustic house or intricate wooden coffering in a Renaissance villa. In its basic guise, a typical Tuscan ceiling is built on a structure of several large beams around 25

ABOVE

Since the Tuscan villa came into fashion in Renaissance times, its situation has been considered even more important than the structure itself. The ideal location was thought to be a hilltop, close to forests and streams for fishing and hunting, and with fields visible beyond.

OPPOSITE

A vine-fringed doorway frames a row of tall cypress trees beside the stone garden wall. These distinctive lines of trees have become synonymous with Tuscany, and despite their appearance as a natural part of the landscape they were in fact planted centuries ago as a way of marking out fields, roadways and property boundaries.

to 30 cm (10 to 12 in) in diameter, running from gable to gable and usually resting on corbels set into the masonry. Running perpendicular to the large beams are numerous smaller beams, around 7 cm (3 in) square. The smaller beams are spaced at a distance of 30 cm (12 in) apart. This supporting frame takes the weight of the ceiling above, generally built from lightweight terracotta bricks. Oak, elm, chestnut or poplar are the traditional woods for ceiling beams. In centuries past, the beams were not planed or squared off, but used in their natural state with the kinks and bends of the tree trunk or branch intact. For villa restorations, these antique beams are sought after for the immediate character they lend to the interior. Oak in particular is prized for its high tensile strength and beautiful grain.

Reflected in vernacular architecture around the world, wood is uniquely suited for ceiling construction. Hardwoods such as oak are very strong: tough enough to provide the necessary support, yet light enough to enable suspension between masonry or brick walls. Stone would be impossible to use in the same way.

In Tuscany, a timber-beamed ceiling may provide an integral strength to the structure of the building, but it is also very beautiful, especially when it is left unpainted in order to show off the knots and colour of the wood. Against a stark white stucco wall or ceiling, the dark stripes of a beamed ceiling take on dramatic qualities. As ever in Tuscany, nature has been tamed and then rearranged in the most appealing way.

In the Tuscan villas of wealthy landowners, wood ceilings have historically also served as a decorative surface. Prior to the Renaissance, the aristocratic country house was relatively simple, its beamed ceilings decorated with ornamental motifs. During the fourteenth and fifteenth centuries, the Tuscan villa became more of a showpiece – consequently, much attention was paid to decoration, and the ceiling became a prime area for aesthetic improvement according to the taste of the day.

During the fifteenth century, wood was used for coffered ceilings in the best houses of Tuscany. These wooden ceilings were compartmentalised into recessed squares, octagons, lozenges and circles, with elaborate carved decoration surrounding each of the shapes. Additionally, gilding and painting might have adorned the wooden surface. From the sixteenth century, stucco became the preferred means of decorating ceilings, but both types of coffering live to this day in palatial villas around Tuscany.

Likewise, flooring trends set during the Renaissance are reproduced in fine country villas, and artisans carry on the traditions of creating refined wooden flooring. In general terms, wooden floors are not especially typical in Tuscany and, if used at all, tend to be on the second level, where wide planks sometimes serve as flooring. This is not only the case with the elegant villas of the wealthy, but also with more rustic dwellings. However, the wooden floor was elevated to an artform in Tuscany during the Renaissance through the techniques of intarsia and marquetry. Again, these same decorative devices continue to be used for floors and furniture in Tuscany nowadays.

Both intarsia and marquetry were used in the Tuscan decoration of the Renaissance period to create a sense of dimensional within the floor, thereby enhancing the feeling of space in a room or hall. Intarsia is a form of inlay that employs thickly cut pieces of wood set into a ground material, while marquetry is a veneer, with thin pieces of wood fitted together over a base of less expensive material to create the effect of a continuous surface. In both cases, different-coloured woods are used to create patterns in the floor. In its most elaborate guise, intarsia could achieve intricate decorative schemes incorporating *trompe l'oeil* effects.

One of the most famous examples of intarsia existed in the choir stalls (which were destroyed by fire in 1749) of the Santo in Pisa. Executed by the renowned artist Lorenzo Canozi, the choir featured the same type of themes and motifs as could be found in the palazzi and country homes of the very wealthy. A visiting Sicilian monk described the intarsia of the Santo as including 'everyday objects, among which are books in intarsia which seem real. Some freshly read and hard to shut … candles … rising smoke … peaches rolling out of a basket.'

Intarsia is obviously a delicate and expensive art, whereas marquetry is more widely seen in Tuscan country homes. In both cost and aesthetic terms, marquetry is far better suited to the vernacular architecture, as it is most commonly applied in the form of geometric patterns repeated across the floor. Both techniques have been used in furniture-making over the past five centuries, and inlaid antique desks, tables and consoles are still popular pieces in the Tuscan interior scheme. They complement the elegant interiors of larger villas and add a touch of refinement to the more rustic interiors of renovated farmhouses.

Intarsia and marquetry – along with other decorative techniques such as panelling and carving – are prominent in the decoration of doors and door surrounds, especially in the splendid country villas of the rich. As always in Tuscany, every architectural element is open to refinement, and doors are no exception. In both simple and more palatial villas, doors provide an opportunity for beautification of the interior.

In farm dwellings, a solid hardwood door needs only to be polished or waxed to make a handsome feature. The warm tones of timber sit well within the whitewashed rooms with their terracotta floors. There is such an abundance of fine wood in Tuscany that it makes sense to show it off rather than paint over or stain it. Even the most opulent room in the grandest villa will have wooden doors, left unpainted and polished, and often featuring inlay or carving to further enhance the colour and grain.

Oak, with its strength, straight grain and light- to dark-

LEFT

Just as the materials of the Tuscan home closely reflect the immediate environment, so too the arrangement of the rooms is designed to harmonise with nature. Rooms for use in summer, such as this open-air living area, usually face north, to give shelter from the sun.

brown tones, is a classic wood for doors, and is also used for other interior purposes such as panelling, flooring and furniture. Beech is abundant in Tuscany and, although not often used in furniture-making, it is the preferred material for kitchen utensils because it is so easy to carve and the wood has no odour or taste. Ceramic or copper containers holding a wide assortment of pale beech ladles are a common sight in farmhouse kitchens.

Just as the Tuscan landscape is typified by lines of tall cypress trees, so architecture and furniture-making in Tuscany is characterised by a distinctive use of cypress wood. Noted for its hardness and durability, cypress is beloved of carpenters and artisans for its superb workability. It is has also been revered as a sacred tree since anicent times: the ancient Egyptians made cypress coffins for mummified kings, whereas the Romans used it for sculptures of their gods. In Tuscany, the cypress is often appropriated as a symbol of the region, and cypress furniture has become a staple of the Tuscan house.

Cypress has a predominantly yellow tone, with hues of red, chocolate or olive. Because of its high oil content, it is very resistant to weathering and is consequently used for exterior doors as well as the window shutters that are such an essential component of the Tuscan villa. Closed against the strong summer sun, they keep rooms shaded and cool.

Shutters and window frames can also be made from chestnut. Tuscany's chestnut groves produce one of the most beautiful woods for all kinds of uses, including the making of wine and oil barrels, and the *bigone*, a container for storing bread. Its distinctive reddish-brown tones make it aesthetically pleasing, and at the same time it is lightweight, easy to split and very resistant to decay. This makes chestnut ideal for external uses, while the wood's straight grain renders it highly suited to furniture-making (indeed, much of the rustic furniture of Tuscany is fashioned from chestnut).

Over the past hundred years, Tuscany's chestnut furniture and stocks of chestnut wood have become prized. North America's once-vast old forests of chestnut have been all but wiped out by blight, and Italy is among those countries that have managed to protect their ancient woods

from the disease effectively.

Perhaps even more valuable than chestnut is walnut wood, which has been used for centuries by Tuscan furniture-makers. Walnut is generally admired for its chocolate colouring, which ranges from mid- to dark brown. It readily lends itself to polishing and has a rich patina that grows more lustrous with age. Walnut has more figures than any other wood, ranging from a straight grain to rhythmic waves and swirls. From a purely practical point of view, it is easily worked.

The tradition of carpentry and carving in walnut dates back to the Renaissance, when some of the most beautiful furniture in Italy was created. In the 1500s the wealthy Florentine nobleman Salvi Borgherini commissioned architect and sculptor Bardemmeo Baglione to design a whole suite of walnut furniture for the bedroom of his son and daughter-in-law. Years later the envoy of Francis I, King of France, attempted to buy the suite for the palace of Versailles. Carved by the master furniture-maker Baccio d'Agnolo, the exquisite

bed and matching cabinets, chests, chairs and settees represent the height of Renaissance artistry. They also attest to the partucular qualities of walnut wood, which lends itslef to being worked with great delicacy.

It is therefore not surprising that such fine furniture has been crafted in Tuscany for generations, when the region's furniture-makers have long benefited from excellent supplies of cypress, chestnut and walnut, among other trees. Although wood is used sparingly in construction, it is used widely in the interior decoration of the villa or farmhouse. Even rustic abodes are furnished with elegant, yet practical, pieces made from chestnut or walnut.

Wooden furniture is a tradition of the region and spans varying styles and periods, from rare carved furniture made by the finest artisans in Florence to the sort of simple country pieces that have been a focus of farmhouse life for centuries. The best pieces are in walnut or chestnut, but pine, elm and poplar are also common. Tuscan furniture tends to be dark in

tone, reflecting the overwhelming use of walnut and chestnut. This toning works to great effect in farmhouses and villas, with their whitewashed walls, reddish-brown terracotta floors and dark ceiling beams. Where pale woods disappear against the strong colouring and dramatic contrasts of the Tuscan interior, the medium to dark grains of walnut, cypress and chestnut look at home. There is some use of the paler woods such as pine and beech, but the darker-coloured woods predominate.

In the Tuscan farmhouse, certain pieces of furniture have remained essential items for centuries. In the grander country villas, meanwhile, changing tastes have seen a variety of proliferating furniture styles. These include: the intricate inlay of multiple woods, as well as inlays of ivory and mother of pearl from the Renaissance; lacquered furniture in the Venetian style of the eighteenth century; the contrived styles of Neoclassical or Empire periods; as well as pretty, painted items from the alpine culture of northern Italy.

Naturally there has been some crossover between the formal, highly decorative furnishings favoured by the wealthy and the simpler pieces of the typical *casa colonica*, but generally speaking the style of farmhouse furniture is little changed. The overriding characteristic of rustic Tuscan furniture is its solidity, but it also displays an attention to detail not usually associated with country furnishings. This is thanks to the Renaissance, when both the newly wealthy and the aristocracy thought it fashionable to live outside of the cities, so long as they could enjoy the same standard of comfort and elegant surroundings accorded by their urban palazzi. The end result is a tradition of furniture-making that blends the simplicity and integrity of living on the land with the harmonious and artistic qualities of the Renaissance. In the same way that the façade of the country villa projects refinement in its symmetrical arrangement of windows, the furnishings also emphasize symmetry, with panelling a common technique.

Rustic furniture (*mobili rustici*) has experienced renewed popularity over the past few decades. Where formal antiques once took pride of place in the country villa, *mobili rustici* has taken their place. The regular antique markets around Tuscany are scoured by well-to-do home owners in search of old farmhouse-style furniture, especially from the sixteenth, seventeenth and eighteenth centuries.

Certain items of furniture have endured in the Tuscan household. In most villas across Tuscany – from the hills above Lucca to the rolling landscape of Chianti – the same basic objects are used in daily life. Rooms are usually sparely decorated, containing a few simple but elegant pieces of wooden furniture.

Storage is one of the primary concerns in any home and, given the lack of built-in storage in the vernacular Tuscan villa, chests and cupboards have become requisite furnishings. The *cassone*, for example, has been an important household item since Renaissance times. Recognised as one of the most common pieces of Tuscan furniture, it is essentially a large, low rectangular storage chest with a hinged lid, and emerged as a characteristic furnishing of the Renaissance (typically crafted from walnut wood). It had several variants: some rested directly on the floor, or on built-in platforms, while others were mounted on four legs, often carved in the shape of lions' paws.

The *cassone* may have started off as a necessity (an item for the storage of one's personal possessions), but through the decorative arts of the Renaissance it became elevated to an article of fine furniture. Almost every chest has different decoration, and the degree of carving, panelling, painting and inlay indicates the wealth and taste of the household that owned it. The fashion for decorated *cassoni* developed during the fifteenth century, when they were given as wedding gifts to members of the aristocracy. Invariably, they bore the family's coat of arms (carved at either end of the chest), or else a symbol associated with the family was incorporated into the overall design. High-relief carving and inlay were the most usual forms of decoration. Painting also became a popular adornment, especially when done in narrative fashion, telling a story that could immediately be comprehended by the viewer.

The wealthiest families commissioned outstanding artists of the day to paint scenes of special relevance on the *cassone*; Giovanni di Paolo and Apollonio di Giovanni were two artists who made a speciality of painting multi-scene narratives on *cassoni*. The trend set by the fashionable rich was emulated at all levels of society, and *cassoni* were found in most households. These typically Tuscan chests are still a staple piece of furniture, and beautifully decorated antique *cassone* (ranging from charmingly rustic to truly inspired) can be found in countless villas and farmhouses.

A variation on the *cassone* is the *cassepanca*, a fantastically versatile piece of furniture that has two practical purposes, serving as both seating and storage. A long bench with a hinged seat that lifts up to reveal storage space, the *cassepanca* is designed for positioning against a wall and it is economical with space. In typically Tuscan fashion, they are usually made from walnut and may be carved and panelled, or inlaid, to create a thing of great beauty.

The cupboard, or *credenza*, is another significant furnishing in the Tuscan house. Usually resting on legs of some kind, the *credenza* is a type of dresser, often meant for the kitchen but also used in the dining room to store ceramics and other tableware. It consists of cupboards in the lower part, with drawers in the centre section and open shelving up above. In keeping with Tuscan ideas about harmony and symmetry, the number and spacing of cupboards below is echoed in the identical number and spacing of drawers above. Also important is the subtle use of panels and carved elements to separate and define the individual components of the cupboard. A sturdy chestnut-wood *credenza*, for example, might incorporate poplar panelling, the two wood tones combining to create a harmonious point of visual interest.

The long table is perhaps the most essential piece of farmhouse furniture. Mealtimes are the key events of daily farm life, and feeding the workers is a priority. Then, as now, every working farm needed a table large enough to seat the labourers working the fields, especially during wheat-threshing time or the wine-harvesting season (*vendemmia*), when big communal lunches would be held outside. Gradually, as the farmhouses were taken over by non-farming residents, the long table

moved inside the house, to find a permanent place in the kitchen or dining room. However, in rural areas across Tuscany it is still common to see a dozen or more people seated outside at a well-worn farmhouse table of oak, cypress or pine, either taking a rest from the work of the *vendemmia* at dusk or simply enjoying a lazy Sunday lunch.

Rustic chairs are simple in form. As with other Tuscan furnishings, their distinguishing feature is the quality of wood used to make them – chestnut, oak or walnut, for example. Seats of peasant-style chairs are woven, with a simple straight back comprising two vertical stiles connected by a couple of horizontal bars. Common decorative touches are turned finials atop the stiles at the back of the chair. Long armrests are another feature of Tuscan chairs, again a legacy of cultured Renaissance design.

Up until the Renaissance, chairs in all but the wealthiest homes were a rarity. Chairs were a symbol of power, so most of the population sat on benches or stools, but as the Renaissance unfolded, chairs became more widely used. Many of the chairs found in Tuscan villas originate from the fifteenth century, when several distinctive styles were produced. Today these beautiful items are a much-prized addition to any villa interior.

The Savonarola and Dante were the first chairs to become widely used in Tuscany during the fifteenth century, and they continue to be reproduced in the antique style. Both are low

LEFT

Timber boards make an unusual choice of flooring for a Tuscan home, and are indicative of foreign stylistic influences. Used here in place of cotto bricks or tiles, the warm wood tones bring a northern European sensibility to the room.

RIGHT

A pair of full length oak shutters flank a French door that opens from the living room to the garden. In ages past they would have routinely been secured at night and on cold days to create a safe, cosy interior. However, in the modern era of glazed windows and central heating they serve more to add character than anything else.

folding chairs based on Roman prototypes. The Dante chair comprises a curved curule (X-shaped leg) at the front and one at the back. A low horizontal back sits on top of the rear curule, with long armrests projecting forward to meet the front curule. The small square seat is usually topped with a cushion. The Savonarola chair is similar in conception, but consists of a number of interlaced staves forming the folding curule shape, and the back features a curved crest. Inlay is very common on Savonarola and Dante chairs.

Whether decorating with antiques or reproduction pieces, the house owner in rural Tuscany has become adept at merging traditional ideas with a sense of modern ease. The dark hues of walnut and chestnut furniture are balanced with pale fabrics in the living room and bedroom, and the heavy shapes of traditional *mobili rustici* are countered with comfortable sofas upholstered in white or light tones. In the bedroom, massive antique walnut beds or more rustic wrought-iron bedsteads are softened with beautiful bedlinen or draped bed canopies.

Just as medieval- and Renaissance-era Tuscans reused Roman building materials and architectural elements, modern Tuscans also perpetuate the art of recycling. They take old farmhouse objects that have outlived their former purpose and give them new uses, or make antique furniture work in a comfortable context. An antique *madia* (bread bin), for example, may serve as a desk. The form of a Dante chair may be replicated in wrought iron for a garden seat, or the lines elongated to make comfortable deckchairs slung with canvas. The Tuscans continue to excel at refining and adapting old ideas to suit their lifestyle, which is never far removed from the textures, colours and materials of the land.

RIGHT

Ceilings in Tuscan houses have traditionally made prominent use of wood. In the grandest houses of the Renaissance, ceilings were often lined with wood that was coffered or beautifully painted. The more common ceiling form is a long oak beam with numerous smaller parallel beams radiating from the central support.

Two different ceiling treatments allow for varying approaches to interior decoration. Dark beams above are balanced by keeping the rest of the room in bright white tones. Where the ceiling has been washed white, there is far greater scope for using colour, without fear of overwhelming the room.

LEFT

In the Tuscan interior, decorative touches can crop up in the most unexpected places. A rustic door reveals an elegant lineage in its beautiful moulding and symmetrical patterning. Such devices for enhancing the villa environment became increasingly widespread as the Renaissance progressed.

LEFT

The long wooden table is the most indispensible piece of furniture in the Tuscan household. It has its origins in bygone days, when the numerous workers on a farm sat down together for lunch, often outdoors.

ABOVE

The natural lines of the oak tree are evident in the beams of this ceiling.

Builders working on farmhouse restorations still endeavour to use oak trunks

and branches that have not been squared off.

OPPOSITE

The farmhouse kitchen has always been the centre of household life in Tuscany. It is still the preferred location for family meals in winter when an open fire provides warmth. A solid, rustic wooden table in pine or oak forms the focal point for many Tuscan kitchens.

RIGHT

No villa kitchen is complete without open shelves for displaying ceramic wares. Shelving may be attached directly to walls or, as here, incorporated into the upper part of an antique dresser.

LEFT

A large open dresser shows off a fine assortment of ceramics, especially the handsome blue and white majolica that is so closely associated with Tuscany.

OPPOSITE

Between cupboards of dark walnut wood, a rack displays a superb array of antique copper pans. These are the traditional cooking utensils of Tuscan kitchens, and still a prized domestic accessory.

The delicacy and beauty of wood carving in Tuscany, and in neighbouring Umbria, dates from the Renaissance. Natural motifs incorporating leaves have proved enduring.

OPPOSITE

Fine quality country antiques are especially prized by affluent Tuscan homeowners. Where once they sought elegant formal furnishings, now the interior mood is more relaxed, dictating rustic period furniture.

RIGHT

Taking pride of place in a villa dining room is an antique bureau, or studio mobile, from central Italy. It exemplifies the Tuscan art of creating deceptively simple furniture. While this piece appears rustic, it is actually very refined in its design and execution.

LEFT

An almost infinite variety of painted finishes, especially in shades of green and blue, has been applied to wooden elements such as doors, window frames and shutters. Although often faded over time, they bring a dash of vibrant colour to the otherwise muted Tuscan exterior palette of grey and beige stone, terracotta brick and gold or ochre stucco. Green and blue are thought to bring a cooling influence in climates where long hot summers prevail.

BELOW

Simple, scrubbed wooden kitchen dressers are staples in the Tuscan house – whether remodelled to accommodate a country-style kitchen sink with brass taps, or painted and then rubbed back to create a charming benchtop for cutting freshly baked bread.

OPPOSITE

A refined austerity pervades this tranquil dining room, with its low ceiling and ancient wooden beams. The table and eight matching chairs are cleverly handcrafted reproductions of nineteenth-century pieces, created in the atelier of Rome-based designer Ilaria Miani, who also has a home in Tuscany

ABOVE

Whether stencilled or applied freehand with a brush, decorative effects are commonly found on wooden furniture such as bureaus, dressers and cabinets. The panels of Tuscan pieces lend themselves well to decoration, with floral motifs among the most popular.

OPPOSITE

Lending classical grandeur to a sombre hallway are a series of wooden columns with carved capitals. Although the capital is more typical of a Corinthian column, the smooth rounded form of the shaft is indicative of the Tuscan style of column, thought to have derived from Etruscan temples, and the simplest of the four classical orders defined by Renaissance architect Vetruvius.

OPPOSITE

Chairs made in Tuscany during the Renaissance depended more on inlay and carving for their decoration than paint effects. From the early 1800s, however, the painted style became increasingly popular in Tuscany, as it did throughout most of Europe. Here, a handsome pair of chairs with carved backs and finials have been embellished with gold details.

ABOVE

Romantic paint effects in pretty colours, often incorporating gilding, became popular in Tuscany during the eighteenth century. The trend for painted furniture had orginated in the north of Italy in the early 1700s, with Venice as the centre for this new art.

ABOVE

An exuberant painted bedstead mixes various styles of surface decoration, including a dado of roses, a trompe l'oeil curtain with tassels and moulded panels with arabesques and urns.

RIGHT

With its repeated emblem of a flower-filled urn, this antique painted cupboard from the town of Lucca loosely follows the Empire style, which dominated Italian interior design during the late eighteenth and early nineteenth centuries.

RIGHT

A wardrobe, or armadio, hand-painted in the typical style of nineteenth-century furniture from the mountainous northern region of Italy. The Italian tradition of painting and lacquering wooden furniture was started by the Venetians in the 1700s, in imitation of objects they had seen from the Far East.

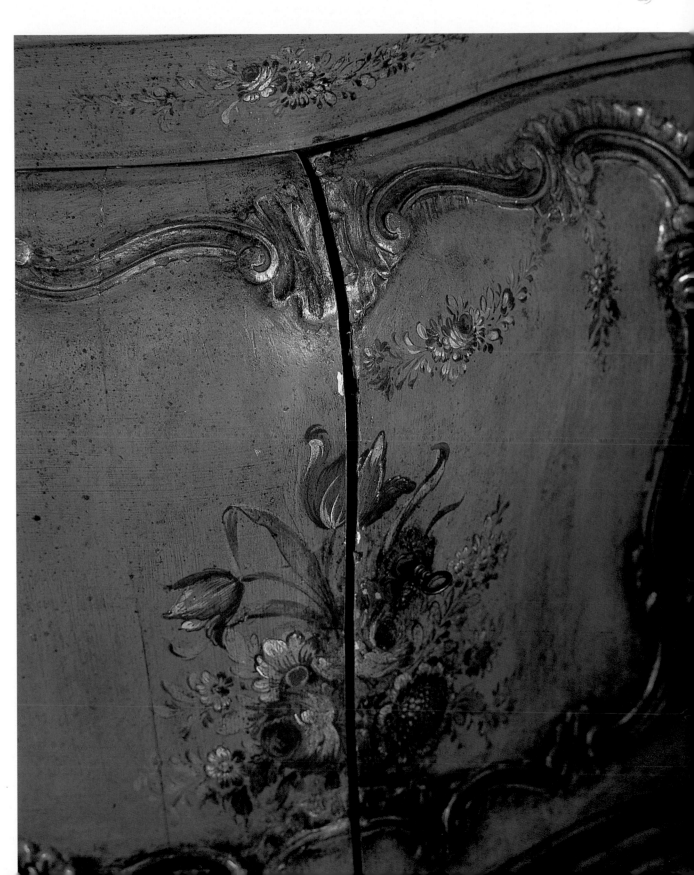

Not all wood-crafted pieces are intended for use on a human scale. This antique miniature theatre is one of a number of eighteenth- and nineteenth-century stages that form the prized collection of a theatre patron. In each set he has recreated scenes from his favourite operas.

RIGHT

An elegant commode in the Empire style of the mid eighteenth century features a curved frontage and carved and gilded scrolling against a background of brilliant blue.

ABOVE

This chest of drawers has been decorated in the manner of brightly coloured furniture from the alpine Alto Adige area of Italy, which borders Austria. The style of embellishment is called arte povera, literally 'poor art' as it was associated with mountain peasants. These days it tends to be as prized in Tuscany as it is now in the north.

OPPOSITE

Drawing on eighteenth-century trompe l'oeil techniques for rendering marble effects, and inspired by northern Italian furniture, interior designer Ilaria Miani has given an imaginative finish to a bureau, part of a matching suite.

BELOW

This example of wooden moulding is testament to the imagination and skill of Tuscan carpenters. Many of heir techniques and ideas have been practised almost continuously for centuries.

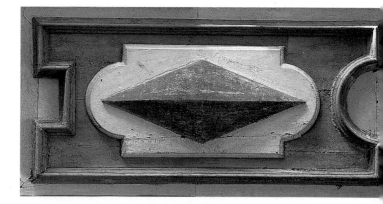

earth

'The charm of certain vacant grassy spaces in Italy, overfrowned by masses of brickwork that are honeycombed by the suns of centuries, is something that I hereby renounce once and for all the attempt to express; but you may be sure that whenever I mention such a spot enchantment lurks in it.'

HENRY JAMES, *ITALIAN HOURS* (1909)

Terracotta is the quintessential colour and texture of Tuscany. Of all the construction elements associated with building in Tuscany, the dusky pink and red hues of this material, of fired unglazed clay, spring most immediately to mind. Indeed, there are few descriptions of the region in any literature that do not mention terracotta; and rightly so – terracotta colouring is prevalent in the architecture and pastoral views of Tuscany. Its warm hue dominates the landscape and the townscapes.

On rooftops, terracotta tiles weather in the sun year after year, fading to pale apricot, rust and gold. On façades, clay bricks project an earthy character, while terracotta friezes and plaques add refinement to even rustic farmhouses. On windowsills, *cassette*, the rectangular window boxes synonymous with Tuscan houses, are filled with red and pink geraniums, while terracotta pots, urns and amphora serve as planting containers in the garden and on terraces and loggias. In outdoor areas, terracotta is also used for paving, its reddish tones serving as an artful counterpoint to pale limestone or grey sandstone walls.

Inside, too, terracotta is found in almost every room. Throughout a farmhouse, townhouse or country villa, flooring of fired clay tile or brick provides a cool surface that seems soft underfoot. A terracotta *battiscopa*, or skirting board, may define the borders of the rooms. In the kitchen, terracotta vessels are used as they have been since Etruscan times for storing oil, wine, cereal and preserved foods. These unglazed earthenwares sit on open shelves or behind wire-covered cupboards alongside colourful majolica ceramics, a different application again of Tuscan terracotta.

As many provincial houses attest, fired clay takes several forms in Tuscany: the bricks so visibly used in the city of Siena as well as other clay building materials; terracotta pots and vessels; the fine majolica made famous in the Renaissance and used for architectural decoration as well as tableware; and the rustic glazed ceramics found in the kitchen of the Tuscan home.

Terracotta is, quite literally, earth (*terra*) that is fired or baked (*cotta*). It is produced in many parts of the world – China, Greece, Japan, the Middle East and India, for example – almost

RIGHT

The rooftops in Tuscan towns and villages, with their terra cotta tiles in hues of burnt orange and brick red, provide the archetypal postcard view. They are one of the key architectural elements of the tuscan region.

LEFT & PREVIOUS PAGE

The beauty of terracotta roof tiles is their ability to age gracefully over the years. They gradually fade from vibrant orange-red to muted shades of ochre and pink, dusted with silvery lichens.

anywhere with a tradition of pottery and the type of clay needed to produce it. Tuscan kiln artisans are fortunate to have access to some of the finest clay in the world, and its particular qualities make it ideal for producing architectural elements such as bricks, tiles and plaques.

The origins of terracotta in Tuscany go back to the Etruscans. Like the ancient Greeks, they learned the craft of pottery and raised it to a fine art. They used it for the obvious things – pots, urns and the like, the terracotta products with which we have become so familiar – but they also incorporated terracotta into the fabric of their buildings. In his musings on the Etruscans, D. H. Lawrence describes this facet of their culture with wonder:

'The Etruscans made small temples, like little houses with pointed roofs, entirely of wood. But then outside they had friezes and cornices and crests of terracotta, so that the upper part of the temple would seem almost made of earthenware, terracotta plaques fitted neatly, and alive with freely modelled painted figures in relief, gay dancing creatures, rows of ducks, round faces like the sun, and faces grinning and putting out a tongue, all vivid and fresh and unimposing.'

On a hill south of Siena, near the town of Murlo, stands Poggio Civitate, a rare Etruscan site with extraordinary remains. It gives some small indication of how widespread the use of terracotta once was. Among the discoveries there in the latter part of the twentieth century were the remains of a kiln, a footprint in an unfired roof tile, along with life-size statues of gods and sphinxes, roof tiles, friezes, plaques with horse-race and banquet scenes, and pottery – all made of terracotta. This rich legacy has provided a fount of ideas and techniques, which Tuscan builders, gardeners, architects and artisans have drawn on for centuries.

The heart of the Etruscan pottery industry was Impruneta. This small town, not far from Florence, still produces the finest terracotta in Tuscany. Many potters consider it the best in the world. Terracotta ovens and brick kilns have been in operation here almost continuously since Etruscan times, and the town's artisans practise a craft that has been passed down through centuries. They still replicate many of the designs from Etruscan, Roman and Renaissance periods. Some of the most experienced artisans do not use a thermometer to monitor the kiln firing. As in Roman times, they can tell when a piece is ready to be removed by the changing colour of the clay. Their skill is one reason for the exalted reputation of terracotta from Impruneta. The other, perhaps and most significant, reason is the quality of the local clay, Galestro.

The chemical composition of Galestro clay makes the terracottas of Impruneta unique. Known locally as *terra turchina*, or blue earth, the clay is coarse and has a very high limestone content. The limestone gives the clay a distinctive golden-pink hue during firing. Galestro can also withstand very high kiln temperatures to produce the only true frost-free terracottas.

They are durable and weather resistant, withstanding temperatures as low as minus 30 degrees Celsius. At the clay pits of Impruneta, twelfth-generation artisans dig grey Galestro clay that is so thick and dense it can be used to make almost any object, no matter how large or how ornate. After being left to weather, the clay is blended to remove any air bubbles that could cause cracking during the firing process. When the clay is ready to use, it is either thrown on a wheel for the making of certain pots and vessels, or packed and pounded into moulds by hand. There are square and rectangular moulds for floor tiles, skirting bands, and other architectural elements with a flat surface. Rounded moulds are used for drainpipes, curved roof tiles and an amazing variety of pots and urns. The moulds are removed once the clay is firm enough and the finishing touches are made by hand.

The unfired objects are left to dry naturally, in the Etruscans – in outdoor sheds, or in rooms maintained at a constant, warm temperature. Left unglazed, the dried pieces are fired at over 980 degrees Celsius. In the furnace of the kiln, the Impruneta clay works its alchemy to form the rich unmistakable colour of terracotta.

Although Galestro clay is the most renowned, it is not the only material for producing Tuscan terracotta. Red clay from Siena is also widely used. Although the Sienese terracottas are not as resistant to cold, they will still withstand temperatures down to minus 10 degrees Celcius, making them well suited to temperate climates. The red terracottas of Siena have a smooth texture and age beautifully. This is the 'fired earth' that gives the city its characteristic colour.

LEFT

The method of laying terracotta roof tiles in Tuscany has been replicated for more than a thousand years, since it was first established by the Romans in ancient times. Two different types of terracotta tile are generally used: the flat, lipped pantile and the overlapping hip pantile, which creates the effect of a series of ridges running from the tip of the roof to the eaves. The alternative and less expensive method is to use only overlapping hip tiles.

OPPOSITE

The faded pinks and golds of the terracotta pantiles above this simple loggia are echoed in the terrace paved with terracotta tiles, the vine-covered brick wall and the fields beyond.

ABOVE

An upper-level window opens directly out onto the eaves of a farmhouse. The colours used for the curtains repeat the mellow beiges and burnt-orange tones of the terracotta tiles. These warm tones tend to dominate the typical Tuscan interior scheme with its peach-coloured stucco walls and wooden furniture in chestnut, oak and pine.

Whether the reddish terracotta of Siena or the pale gold terracotta of Impruneta, their application in Tuscan architecture and interior decoration is almost identical across the region. One of the oldest applications of terracotta is the curved tile, or pantile, that covers the roof of nearly every farmhouse and villa in Tuscany. The pantile, which has an S-shaped cross-section, has been used since Roman times. The system of laying roof tiles also generally follows the Roman model: with a flat, lipped pantile (called *tegola*) placed directly on top of the pitched roof, and then overlapped by a semi-circular hip pantile (called *coppi).

Also used since Roman times are terracotta floor tiles. Unlike the pantiles for roofing, floor tiles are not only a functional building element; they are also chosen for their tactile and aesthetic qualities. Once rubbed with natural wax and buffed, they become soft to the touch, a sensual surface for walking on with bare feet.

Available in a wide range of colour tones and sizes, terracotta floor tiles bring a distinctive visual character to the Tuscan house. In the simplest application, as large tiles uniformly laid, their warm pink casts a soft glow around the room, reflecting off whitewashed walls or ceiling. Used in more sophisticated ways, the variety of terracotta hues and tile shapes can be enhanced in the laying of patterned floors.

The trend for patterned tile flooring was set during the Renaissance. Terracotta tiles were manufactured in square, rectangular and hexagonal shapes and laid in a variety of geometric patterns: in a herringbone pattern, which had been used widely by the Romans; in parallel lines; or rectangular frames repeated all over the floor. Tilers in Tuscany still lay these same patterns, exploiting the subtle colour differences between terracotta tiles to maximise the effect of the patterning.

A variation on the thin terracotta tiles is *cotto*, the rough-hewn terracotta bricks used for flooring in the rustic *casa colonica*. Although more inexpensive than the finer terracotta tiles, and traditionally used in more humble dwellings, even *cotto* are laid with aesthetics in mind, often in a herringbone pattern. As in Renaissance times, bricks for flooring are available in various textures such as ribbed, rough or glazed. At their most beautiful they are worn smooth over time and polished with wax to bring out their deep red colour.

There is a lively trade in used tiles and *cotto*, rescued from old buildings slated for demolition or which have simply been neglected and crumbled over the years. The patina and smoothness of this ancient terracotta flooring can only be achieved over years of wear, and so it is much sought after for villa restorations.

Other uses for terracotta are evident on the façades of houses. Villas might feature a terracotta frieze above a doorway, or plaque on the wall, even terracotta columns. A family coat of arms, or *stemme*, in glazed or unglazed terracotta is a popular personal form of decoration on some houses.

Drainage pipes are another feature often beautifully wrought in terracotta – a typically refined Tuscan treatment of a purely functional architectural element. Thick terracotta tiles may be laid across the top of a stone retaining or garden wall, creating a smooth ledge where fruits and tomatoes are left out to dry in the sun ready for preserving, or where geranium-filled pots make a colourful display.

Likewise, terracotta tiles are used to finish windowsills, both inside and outside the window frame. This is especially noticeable in the deep window recesses of upstairs rooms. When looking at the house from a distance, the terracotta edge of the windowsill draws a neat defining line, emphasising the window opening. As an alternative to the stone window ledge, terracotta tile brings warm tones and a sense of lightness to the façade of the house.

Aside from the terracotta tiles and mouldings that come in so many forms, terracotta brick is an essential building element. Since Roman times it has been used for construction on a grand scale, and since the Renaissance it has been used as a decorative material to bring definition and colour to stone and stuccoed houses. Unlike stone with its strength and mass, brick appeals on a much more personal scale. If made by hand, brick bears the mark of the maker's hands. Its smaller size makes it somehow seem more delicate, and the nature of bricklaying means it can be easily used to make patterns. However it is made, and in whichever pattern it is laid, the terracotta brick, with its characteristic pink colouring, immediately draws attention.

The history of brick manufacture in Italy dates back to Roman times. Brick-making in its simplest form used the sun to slowly bake the clay until hard. The Romans, who required huge amounts of building material for their grand construction projects, further refined the process and built kilns aimed at mass production.

Brick manufacture was a sizeable industry in ancient Rome, providing the means for rapid and economical expansion of the city and its empire. Rich landowners invested in brick kilns, taking advantage of the pool of labour at their disposal. The emperors, too, were aware of the money to be made when demand for building materials was expanding, and they owned some of Rome's largest brickyards.

Long after the fall of Rome, Roman-made bricks were recycled in new buildings across Europe. Even the Normans drew on supplies of ancient Roman brick when they began building their churches in England in the eleventh century. The technique of brick manufacture lived on, too, providing subsequent generations with the basis for a thriving brick industry. Italy pioneered the brick industry, and there is more evidence of early brick manufacture and architecture in medieval Italian towns than almost anywhere else in Europe.

Although there was abundant stone and marble in Tuscany it did not always suit the needs of builders and architects to

OPPOSITE

In certain parts of Tuscany, especially around Siena and in the hilltowns, brick is a predomiant feature of the architecture. Brick manufacture in this area of Italy dates to Roman times, and became especially popular during the building boom of the Renaissance, as stone and marble were heavy and expensive to transport. Brick, on the other hand, could be produced inside the city walls, or even on the site of large building projects.

ABOVE LEFT

The typical pink-red bricks used to such great visual effect in Siena take their colour from the rich clays of the region. Brick is still made in Tuscany and continues to be used for all kinds of structures from major building works to a simple garden wall – here rendered in a mid-twentieth-century style with insets of terracotta pipe.

ABOVE RIGHT

Two forms of terracotta tradition are displayed in this garden wall. The rough texture of handmade brick represents the purely functional output of Tuscany's kilns, while the terracotta gargoyle set into the wall is testament to the sculptural skills of the kiln artisans. Masks like this date from the age of Mannerism and continue to be reproduced today.

use it. Brick was a comparatively cheap building material. Unlike stone and marble, which were costly and difficult to transport, brick was light and inexpensive, and could be made in kilns not too far from a city's building works. Siena and Florence in particular used brick extensively.

To begin with, brick was viewed primarily as a utilitarian building material, with little intrinsic aesthetic value. By the end of medieval times and the beginning of the Renaissance, Florence was almost entirely made from brick. But the brick used in buildings was usually covered with a cladding of stone or marble, or with a layer of stucco, so the distinctive terracotta colour and texture was scarcely visible at all. It was only later, during the Renaissance, that brick was used for its visual effect. There was a transition to building in brick for aesthetic reasons and masons developed a distinct brick architecture. Palazzo Grifoni, built in 1557, is one of the first examples of brick being used in a major façade for intentional decorative purposes.

One of the single most outstanding brick features in Tuscany is the cathedral dome in Florence, devised by the Renaissance architect Filippo Brunelleschi. The workshops at Impruneta provided him with the bricks he needed in 1420 to commence construction of the cupola of the Santa Maria del Fiore. Brunelleschi had been inspired by the Romans, who developed herringbone-style brickwork – still seen in the vernacular architecture of Tuscany. In those days, the Impruneta brick kilns were as renowned as they are today, but there were also numerous other brickworks around Tuscany.

Some of the first permanent brick kilns were established in Florence, just outside the city gates. They were well developed, designed to produce on a mass scale. As established in the statutes of 1325, the standard brick was the *mattone*, with a fixed size of about 28 cm (11 in) long, 15 cm (6 in) wide and 7.5 cm (3 in) thick. Later on, two other types of official brick were introduced: the *quadruccio*, which was a little narrower than the *mattone*; and the *mezzana*,

ABOVE

Typical of Tuscan façades, the exterior of this house combines brick, stucco and wood. From the Renaissance onwards, brick and other forms of terracotta detail were often used as decorative elements to edge doorways and windows. Drawing attention to the doors and windows in this way helped to emphasise the symmetry of the façade.

As opposed to stone, brick was an ideal material for constructing the terraced houses of the hill towns. Brick enabled quick and easy erection of tall houses arranged along steep lanes, while still allowing the inclusion of elegant arcaded façades.

OPPOSITE & LEFT

As the tastes and fortunes of Tuscans changed over the centuries, their homes were adapted accordingly, with the additon of more rooms or the layering of building materials over the façade. Applying stucco over brick and stone was a common means of shoring up ageing walls and protecting them from the elements, as well as creating a lighter asethetic. Over time, the stucco, too, would become worn away to reveal the building's architectural history.

which was wider but thinner than the *mattone*. Each brickyard was required to display a model brick mould – bound in iron and stamped with a government seal – and there were heavy penalties for flouting the regulations. Because of the industrial nature of their work, and its importance to the city, kilnsman operated under much stricter controls than other artisans did. Their work was also amongst the toughest of any trade. The Florentine wit Piovano Arlotto joked that kilnsman were the cleanest people in the city – because they alone washed their hands before going to the toilet.

For reasons of safety, kilns were not commonly found in the city itself. They were generally located outside the city walls, beside the clay pits that provided the raw material. Working the clay was an important part of the whole process. Once dug, it had to be weathered before being moulded into bricks ready for firing. The great Renaissance architect and commentator Leon Battista Alberti, who made intensive studies of the trades, advised that clay should be dug in the autumn, weathered through the winter, then moulded into bricks in the spring and fired. Today, little has changed in the methods used by the kiln workers and artisans of Impruneta.

There are few examples of terracotta brickwork more impressive than the city of Siena, which is built almost entirely from red brick. Although brick was used early on in Florence as well, from the Renaissance Florence began to make much wider use of stone. Siena's ruling body made a decision to redevelop the city centre using brick, precisely because it would stand out from its rival. However, there were other reasons for choosing brick. Stone would have been very expensive to transport from distant quarries, whereas brick was produced just outside the city walls. Brick also served an important aesthetic purpose.

When it was completed in 1347 one chronicler of the time wrote that the Campo '… is held to be one of the most beautiful of all squares which can be seen not only in Italy bit in the whole of Christendom, both for the loveliness of the fountain and for the beauty of the buildings which surround it.' The city fathers were so impressed with the outcome of the Campo, they ordered that brick should be used in all new houses in Siena. The Sienese recognised an important principle that has filtered down to influence vernacular Tuscan architecture and interior decoration: that architectural unity can be achieved through colour and material alone. In the case of Siena, the brownish-red of terracotta brick (the colour we now call 'burnt sienna') gives the main square, the Campo, its impressive visual impact. Applied at a domestic level, this certainly rings true in the Tuscan countryside.

The warm hues of Tuscan brick crop up everywhere in domestic architecture. In Siena, of course, and in other instances scattered throughout Tuscany, houses are constructed entirely from brick. Even when stone is the predominant building material, bricks are often incorporated into the stone walls of many old *casa colonica*. As these ancient farmhouses have evolved over the years, builders have turned to whatever material they could find to build new walls or shore up old ones. This often meant using brick, because it was cheap and could even be made on the farm premises, or because it had been recycled from some old ruin of a house, possibly even a Roman one. In addition, bricks are sometimes employed at the corners of walls instead of stone quoins. Usually for reasons of economy, but often just as much for visual impact, stepped terracotta bricks are laid to mark and strengthen the junction of two walls.

However, by far the most common usage of brick on façades is when incorporated together with stone as a material for definition. In Renaissance times, architecture was clean and decisive, with elements arranged in a logical and pleasing fashion. Achieving harmony was the key aim of architects and builders, and it became particularly important for the façade to impart a sense of symmetry. Brick became a useful and attractive material for enhancing this symmetry, by emphasising the placement of doors, windows and other entry points to the house. This aesthetic has remained the dominant one in Tuscany, and had been applied to all but the lowliest buildings.

Terracotta bricks are used to frame doorways, edge window frames, and decorate the arches of a loggia. This is seen all over Tuscany. In the hill towns, the repeated use of brick to define doors and windows helps to unify entire streets of terraced houses. It is used to create arched openings in stone walls and borders around windows, to support houses built over alleyways, and to reinforce older stone walls.

Out in the countryside, touches of brickwork add refinement to the stone façades of traditional farmhouses and villas. Tracing the arches of a loggia, a thick, single row of bricks, set on their ends, projects upward into the stone wall to provide a neat finish. Sometimes the row of bricks continues down to ground level to create a bridge effect; or otherwise simply etches the curve of the arch. In some cases, an additional row of terracotta tiles may be set above, projecting beyond the brick, to add a decorative rim to the arch.

A similar treatment is repeated around doorways and windows. Where the openings are arched, such as in a loggia, a row of bricks is set to trim the edge of the curve. If the openings are square or rectangular in shape, the brick is typically set into the stone in a gentle arch six inches or so above, creating the effect of a brow above the opening. From a distance, the terracotta brick elegantly marks out the façade of the house, yet is subtle enough to blend beautifully with the stone or stuccoed exterior.

Indoors, too, terracotta brick serves two functions. It is an essential material for rendering structural elements, but at the same time its texture, colour and patterning make a decorative addition to the Tuscan interior. One legacy of the Renaissance

ABOVE

The glazed shine of a ceramic jug contrasts with the powdery texture of a terracotta brick wall. Just as the production of Tuscan terracotta developed into a prosperous industry, so too did the making of glazed ceramics, which grew into a fine art. Both products draw on the same high-porosity clays.

RIGHT

Brick has been historically used for vast building projects because it is so easy to work with and relatively cheap to produce. By the late Middle Ages and early Renaissance, there was a well organised system of brick manufacture, controlled by a powerful guild. Most large buildings were made from brick, covered with a layer of stucco or stone.

OPPOSITE

A medieval Italian style of window, called bifore, *with its dividing column and twin arches is given a distinctive Tuscan treatment. The window is set mainly in brick but the refined manner of framing incorporates touches of stone and marble which are evident in the windowsill, the corbels supporting the arch above, and in the column itself.*

ABOVE

Terracotta bricks are used to transform a plain stuccoed wall into a point of aesthetic interest. Brick was originally used in Tuscany as a basic building material, to be covered with stone or stucco, in cities such as Florence. But in Siena brick was purposefully used for visual impact and left uncovered. As the Renaisssance unfolded, brick became increasingly used as an architectural device employed for surface decoration.

is the stylistic concern that all surfaces of the room should be co-ordinated into an interior scheme. Thus the ceiling design should ideally match that of the floor, with the same spatial divisions employed.

Echoing the *cotto* that typically surfaces the floor, the ceiling can also incorporate bricks to dramatic effect, fulfilling the Renaissance desire for co-ordination. A vaulted brick ceiling is therefore a prized feature of a villa or *casa colonica*. The most common type of vaulted ceiling is the barrel, or tunnel vault, which is, as its name suggests, like the roof of a tunnel – a smooth concave shape. Made of terracotta brick laid in either parallel lines or a herringbone pattern to replicate the *cotto* flooring, the vaulted ceiling lends a remarkable refinement and harmony to the room. This thoughtful application of simple building materials is typical of the way in which rustic Tuscan architecture works to convey an overall impression of beauty and elegance, without resorting to showy displays.

The colour of terracotta used inside the home is the inspiration for the wide range of earth-toned stuccoes that often cover walls and ceilings. If interior walls are not whitewashed, the popular choice is for a pale-apricot or ochre-coloured plaster so that walls and floors appear to blend, with the definition between them becoming less obvious. This can be a purposeful way of enhancing the size of a room and minimising the effect of low ceilings, especially in some older farmhouses. Terracotta brick and tile crop up in other aspects of the interior, typically in a minor role but nevertheless adding a touch of handmade character. A fireplace of brick or stone is usually edged with terracotta tiles, and the brick chimney may also be revealed as a feature. In the kitchen, too, terracotta tiles are used atop benches and to line niches and shelves. Here they serve as a sturdy surface as well as repeating the colour of the *cotto* floor. A brick oven may take pride of place in large farmhouse kitchens, and be used to make pizza and bread as in centuries past.

Essential to the Tuscan kitchen is the comforting presence of terracotta storage urns and glazed terracotta kitchenwares. Since Etruscan times, olive oil and wine have been stored in terracotta vessels. Particularly in the case of olive oil, storage in terracotta keeps it cool and protected from the light, which can cause it to spoil. There are a wide variety of terracotta designs for liquid storage – from small oil vessels with cork stoppers to larger amphora and urns, sometimes fitted with little brass taps to dispense the contents. For other types of comestibles, too, terracotta containers abound.

Alongside the earthy tones of unglazed, or clear-glazed, terracotta, most Tuscan kitchens display some of the colourful ceramics of the region. These ceramics are made from the same clay as terracotta but are glazed and decorated to create a glossy surface with rich bright colours. The most famous of Tuscan ceramics is majolica, a terracotta pottery that is coated in a tin glaze and fired to create a dense white surface ideal for painting. The principal colours for decoration are cobalt blue, green, purple, brown, yellow and orange, and motifs range from simple floral and oak-leaf patterns to elaborate historical and mythological scenes.

Originating in the Middle East and spreading far across Europe, majolica reached Italy in the fifteenth century. In Renaissance Tuscany, majolica emerged as one of the most beautiful crafts of the age, and one that continues to live on through the numerous potteries that reproduce traditional designs. Because the maiolica of Tuscany is made from terracotta, the tin glazing is a critical step in order to mask the red pigment and create an opaque white background for decorating. It is a challenge that has been masterfully overcome by some of the finest craftsmen and artists in Italy's history.

The artist given credit for making Tuscan majolica so revered is Luca della Robbia. At his family pottery in the fifteenth century he produced plates and pots of exceptional beauty and individuality. Perhaps even more importantly, he pioneered the use of multicoloured glazed terracotta for architectural use – for reliefs, for doorway tympanum (between the lintel and the arch above) and decorative medallions, for tombstones, fountains and altars. His ideas and designs, especially his combination of blue and white, have been much emulated over the centuries. Evidence of della Robbia's legacy is seen in many Tuscan homes: in the ceramic plaques mounted beside front doors; in the ceramic planters in the garden; in ceramic sinks and fountains. Majolica floor tiles, originally used for only the villas and urban palazzos of the wealthy, are widely appreciated and used both inside and outside.

During the Renaissance, majolica objects were exclusive and expensive, usually the domain of the wealthy. From the mid seventeenth century, cheaper types of maiolica with simpler decoration made the ceramic far more accessible. From a fine art it has become predominantly a folk art. Although now a common part of Tuscany's material culture, in the fifteenth century this architectural application of terracotta seemed truly new and daring.

As Impruneta is to unglazed terracotta products, so Montelupo is to majolica. Since the fifteenth century, the workshops at Montelupo have continued to generate a huge variety of majolica objects, from dinner sets to floor tiles. Majolica is a blending of art and utility, making it perfectly suited to the gentile environment of the Tuscan villa.

Any discussion of terracotta would not be complete without reference to the garden. On windowsills, in loggias and in courtyards, tubs and pots filled with bright flowers are decorative features beloved of the Tuscans. They are adept at bringing a sense of the outdoors inside. This idea of taming nature, adapting it to a human scale yet maintaining a sense of spontaneity and charm, has been part of Tuscan culture for centuries. Many of the same objects used in landscaping the Tuscan home environment, such as window boxes and garden pots, are ubiquitous throughout the Mediterranean, yet Tuscany remains unrivalled in the quality and artistry of its terracotta craft. The excellent clays of the region make frost-free terracottas, withstanding very cold temperatures without cracking. This of course makes them ideal for use outside in the garden. The mineral content of the clay causes them to age beautifully, gradually taking on a gently weathered character and silky texture.

Tuscan terracotta has excellent porosity and pots are usually given a good soaking before they are planted so that the plant's root system does not have to compete with the pot for water. Once established, the potted plant thrives within the porous terracotta.

There is an extraordinary array of pots and containers for planting. Boxes, or *cassettas* for windows and courtyards usually feature some motif in relief, from a simple swag or garland to mythological figures and scenes from the classics. There are low circular pots, or *vaso*, decorated with a simple doube ridge, or with a garland motif; or pitchers, *orcio*, which are taller and swell out around the middle.

For attaching to garden and courtyard walls there are semi-circular wall containers, *tasca*, with ridges, scallops or more ornate designs in relief. *Lavello*, or wall-mounted basins, with taps or spouts are another characteristic piece of garden furniture. Other terracotta objects are used purely for decoration in the garden, a statue of a lion, or of a figure from Greek or

Roman mythology; or urns mounted on pedestals. The practice of gardening in terracotta pots is well suited to the Tuscan villa. In medieval times the garden supplied food for the household: lemons and oranges, pears, apricots, figs, olives almonds and more. By the Renaissance, the new generation of villa owners using their homes solely as a retreat had small enclosed gardens built adjoining the house. This garden was simply a place where the residents could take time to reflect and admire the beauty of nature. In this controlled environment, large terracotta pots were the perfect accessory.

In the Tuscan garden, terracotta is appreciated as much for its ornamental as for its practical value. In its ability to merge the organic beauty of nature with the architectural qualities of a man-made object, it is unmatched. And its influence on the look and feel of the Tuscan house is palpable: both indoors where the colour of *cotto* floors dictates the interior scheme, and outdoors where it serves to define the shape and structure of a façade. Terracotta embodies the fusing of function and form, of craft and refinement that have sustained Tuscan architecture and culture for centuries.

ABOVE

The Renaissance qualities of harmony and symmetry are strikingly displayed in an arcaded terrace with columns of red brick.

RIGHT

The golden colours of terracotta come to life as the warm afternoon sunlight illuminates a portico made of brick and paved with rough cotto. *In the garden beyond, the old well has been restored.*

ABOVE

A windswept autumn courtyard is paved in terracotta bricks laid in parellel lines. Several terracotta garden pots decorate the space, but the centrepiece is a massive urn that once was used to hold olive oil or wine. This type of terracotta vessel dates from ancient Roman days.

OPPOSITE

Terracotta tiles and bricks are usually laid in a variety of geometric patterns, to enhance differences in colour and texture. The herringbone pattern used to pave this outdoor terrace was widely used in Roman times and became popular again during the Renaissance.

LEFT

The traditional terracotta tiles of Tuscany, made by hand, are immediately recognisable for their slight unevenness and their colour variation. These tonal differences reflect the mineral content of local clays.

Terracotta tiles weather beautifully over time, and antique examples have become a prized feature of the Tuscan farmhouse. Alternatively, there are numerous kiln works in the region producing new terracotta tiles, either fashioned to replicate a worn-in patina or glazed to give a polished look.

LEFT

Terracotta urns and pots were once crafted by the Etruscans to hold liquids and grain, but are now used primarily for gardening. The enclosed courtyards and terraces of the Tuscan house are ideally suited to this type of container planting.

ABOVE

Massive terracotta jars like this one are still produced in potteries throughout Tuscany. Traditionally used for storage they are now more often found in the garden setting – as containers for citrus trees and flowering shrubs, or simply as a striking ornament.

ABOVE & RIGHT

The reds and pinks of terracotta provide the inspiration for exterior and interior colour schemes. Stucco, tinted with the colours of Tuscan clay, has been in use for centuries to protect and seal external brick walls, and to render interior walls.

LEFT

This charming scene conveys Tuscan living at its most gracious, a mix of modern and traditional influences. The fresh apricot colour of the walls is echoed, and even exaggerated, by pretty floral cushions in hues of gold and amber, a fringed orange throw and a small pink lamp.

BELOW

A magnificent vaulted ceiling constructed from brick gives this living room a sense of great spaciousness. The texture and tone of the brick ceiling is repeated in the pale pink flooring of cotto.

OPPOSITE

The warm earth tones of terracotta floor tiles and pale golden stucco create a suitably rustic backdrop for a simple wooden bench, weathered clay pots and an antique rack hung with straw sunhats.

OPPOSITE

A massive wood-fired oven dominates this farmhouse kitchen. On either side of the oven, open shelving displays a cheerful clutter of baskets, cooking utensils and ceramics, including unglazed terracotta and glazed tableware.

ABOVE

The archetypal elements of the farmhouse kitchen are captured here – a string of shiny onions hanging against an aged stuccoed wall, and a cluster of vivid green and red chillis pinned to a rough wooden column. Both are essential ingredients for the Tuscan cook.

LEFT

Friezes, mouldings and medallions sculpted from terracotta are distinctive architectural features of Tuscany. The Etruscans were among the first civilisations to use fired clay for this type of external decoration, and the fashion was revived again in fifteenth-century Italy where terracotta friezes became a favoured device of Renaissance architects.

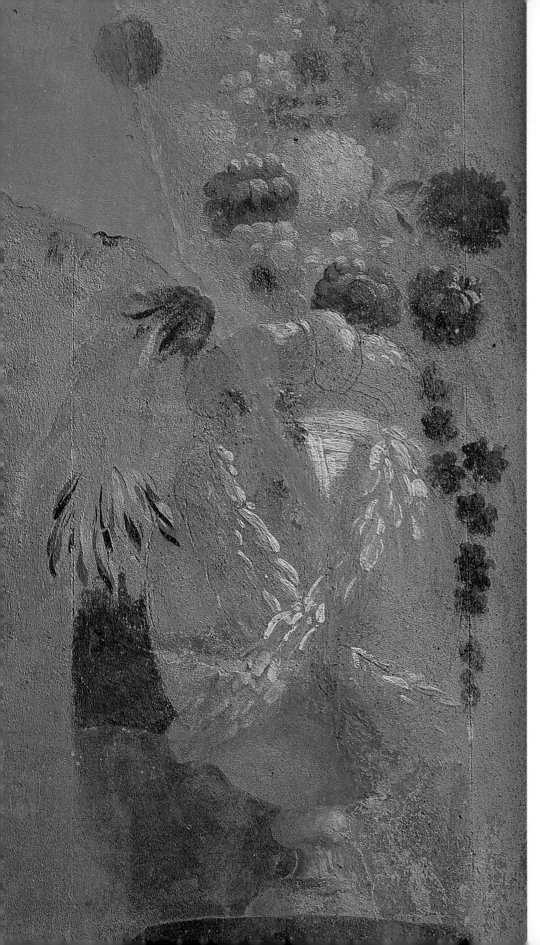

LEFT & RIGHT

Delicate frescoes in subdued colours render naturalistic subjects in a romantic style. This form of decoration was very popular during the Renaissance, and it continues to be a typical treatment of earth-toned stucco walls, in Tuscany, to this day.

RIGHT

Clay tones create a sense of warmth and informality in this sun-drenched interior. The colour scheme is the perfect counterpoint to the grand proportions of the rooms and elegant antique furnishings.

BELOW

A farmhouse staircase is given an unusual treatment, with a graphic pattern of alternating triangles in cream and pale ochre painted on each riser. The colours were created using only natural pigments to create a soft, sheer wash.

ABOVE

This bedroom takes the strong pinks of terracotta as its starting point to create a vibrant backdrop painted ina pigment-rich wash. To balance the dramatic rose-coloured walls, the rest of the room is essentially free of colour. A black wrought-iron bed, a typically Tuscan piece of furniture, is covered with a romantic white bedspread.

LEFT & ABOVE

The prolific production of terracotta garden pots around Tuscany means that most gardens, no matter how humble, are stocked with a generous supply of basins, pots and urns for planting with herbs, flowers or small fruit trees.

RIGHT

Figurative statuary – whether in terracotta, marble or stone – is an essential ingredient in the Tuscan garden. The trend for garden statues, particularly of mythological figures, became firmly established during the Renaissance.

LEFT

Sculpted terracotta finials decorate the top of a garden wall surrounding a limonaia, or lemon house, at the seventeenth-century Villa i Cotrozzi. The finials are original and are typical of the refined garden designs of Tuscany.

BELOW

This classical scene incorporates all the elements associated with the Tuscan villa: a façade of creamy-beige stucco, with windows and doorway symmetrically arranged and edged with pale grey stone; terracotta pots planted with trees and colourful geraniums; and a terracotta statue in the garden depicting a figure from mythology.

OPPOSITE & BELOW

When glazed, the mineral-rich clays of Tuscany take on a rich caramel colour and smooth surface, in contrast to the dusty reds and matt texture of unglazed terracotta. The first guild of terracotta masters was founded in 1308 in the famous pottery town of Impruneta.

RIGHT

A terracotta urn sits in a brick-edged niche set within a rough stone wall. This primitive form of storage keeps the contents of the urn cool and protected from the sun's rays.

RIGHT

The generous scale of Tuscan pottery makes it ideal for holding the hearty dishes of the region. Here, an autumnal dish of beans is served in a large rustic-style earthenware bowl. Some earthenware can also be used for cooking on the stovetop – for easy transfer directly to the table.

BELOW

The two forms of Tuscan pottery – glazed and unglazed – meet in this lipped bowl, creating a delightful contrast between the rough and the refined. The inside is lined with a creamy-yellow glaze, while the outside is pink terracotta.

OPPOSITE

The characteristic colours of majolica are embodied in this decorative plate: white, cobalt blue, antimony yellow and a ferrous orangey-yellow. Although inspired by much earlier pottery from Islamic Mesopatamia, the ceramics known as majolica originated in Tuscany in the fifteenth century.

RIGHT

Tuscany has attracted Italians from all over the country, bringing with them decorative styles and furnishings from elsewhere. This elaborately tiled stove, or stufa, for example, is typical of the Italian alps.

ABOVE

Colourful majolica tiled floors have been popular in Tuscany since the Renaissance. The inlay of family crests and coats of arms is another stylistic device from the same period. This flooring design uses deep blue and yellow on a white background to striking effect.

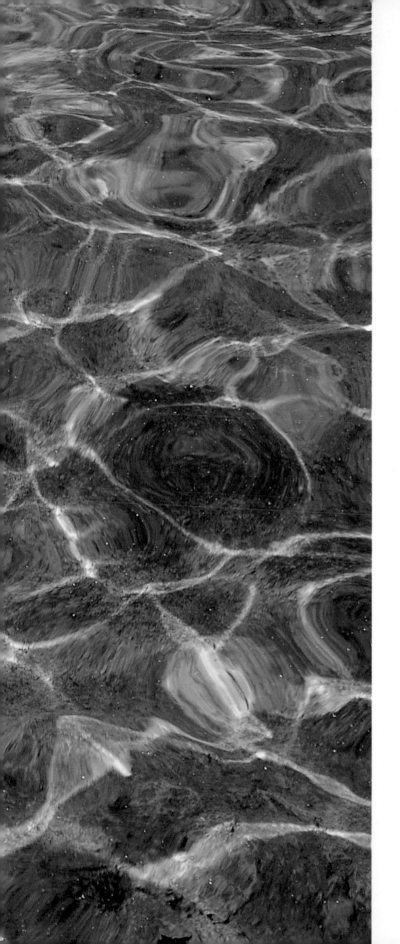

water

'The house is a square of four pavilions…and the gardens are delicious, and full of fountains.'

JOHN EVELYN (1645)

The materials associated with Tuscan landscape and architecture are overwhelmingly earthy in tone, colour and texture: rough golden stone, burnt-red terracotta, warm-hued chestnut, oak and walnut wood. The transient and mercurial element of water is an unexpected addition to this mix, yet it is one that completes the scene of Tuscan living. Although water comprises the smallest and most subtle component of Tuscan architecture, it is an intrinsic part of it nevertheless.

No villa or farmhouse is complete without a fountain, pond or pool. Water may be present in a minute scale, lying still in the perfect curve of a white marble basin, or it may be used on a vast scale, to fill a deep-blue swimming pool overlooking rolling hills and fields. Either way, water provides the necessary elemental balance to the earthbound quality of country life in Tuscany. Entirely aside from the man-made features that appear in the landscape, in gardens, on terraces and in courtyards, water is very much a part of Tuscany's geography.

Hundreds of thousands of years ago, the land was covered by large lakes. The coastal strip lay deep underwater and only the highest points rose out of the water as islands (the sites of present-day Siena, Piombino, Monte Argentario, and the hills behind Lucca and Livorno). The rocks here still contain fossils of fish, shells and coral – as the sea receded and the lakes dried up, great rivers formed, building up silt in the lower altitudes to form the Tuscan plains. Along the coast, the receding ocean deposited sand and clay, which became marshland.

Nature has therefore endowed the region with abundant supplies of water. The Apennine mountains that dominate the Tuscan horizon supply a network of torrential rivers that wind across the region. The Reno, Santerno, Lamone, Marecchia and Foglia rivers make their way to the Adriatic, while the Tiber, the Arno and its many tributaries – the Cecina, Ombrone and Albegna rivers – flow to the Tyrrhenian Sea. In the course of their journey, these waterways feed the fields and vineyards of Tuscany, and make their presence clear in the landscapes and townscapes.

For all the architectural splendours of Florence, the city's position on the Arno is its defining characteristic. Few writers praising the beauty of the city have escaped mention of the river

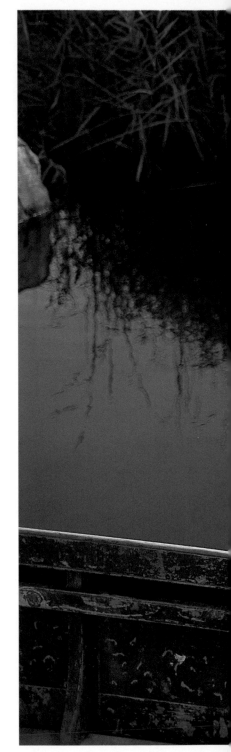

RIGHT

The element of water plays a subtle yet important part in the Tuscan living environment. Its cooling presence is a source of comfort during the hot summer days that are so typical of central Italy.

running through its midst; indeed, English poet Elizabeth Barrett Browning described Florence as 'the most beautiful of cities, with the golden Arno shot through the breast of her like an arrow'. The combination of man-made splendour and water (nature's most powerful and essential force) is irresistible. This idea also underpins the age-old inclusion of water as a feature of Tuscan houses.

Like stone, wood and earth, water is a vital part of any household. It is required for washing, bathing, sewage and irrigation. The latter two functions do not manifest themselves obviously in the aesthetics of the house, but as washing and bathing take place in a dedicated space – the bathroom – the containment and use of water necessarily become considerations in the interior design of the Tuscan house. In keeping with its purpose as a place of cleansing and purification, where the naked bather returns to a state of nature, the archetypal Tuscan bathroom pulls together all the raw elements typically found in the vernacular architecture: stone, wood, earth and water.

At its most luxurious, the element of stone may be present in a bath or washbasin of white and pale-grey Carrara marble, or in a marble counter. In sparsely decorated bathrooms, a marble cup or dish might sit atop the washbasin or benchtop. Striking a more rugged note, a perfectly simple Renaissance stone sink may be plumbed in against one wall, with a bronze faucet dispensing water from above.

The warm colour of wood also appears in the bathroom, perhaps with the judicious placement of a farmhouse-style chair made from chestnut. As elsewhere in the house, wooden beams define the ceiling. Earth is present in the terracotta tiles or *cotto* bricks that usually line the bathroom floor, and serve in place of shiny glazed tiles to edge the bath or shower. All is kept plain and natural, with matt, textured surfaces. Reclining in a bathtub filled with hot water, illuminated by the flicker of candlelight, the bather cannot help but be soothed by the charming simplicity of the rustic Tuscan bathroom.

The other internal area where water plays an important role is the kitchen,. Here, the sink is a matter of pride for the householder. Stainless-steel and modern coated sinks are banished in favour of an old-fashioned, characterful look. The owner may be lucky enough to track down a large rectangular marble sink (perhaps of Carrara marble), on which there are numerous variations. It may come with its own matching marble splashback set with bronze faucets, or, if sourced from one of the old monasteries, the sink might be long enough to fit against an entire wall, with several sets of faucets. Equally appealing, and perhaps more practical, a plain white, rectangular ceramic sink fulfils its function of providing water while still complementing the rustic interior.

Inside, water is generally restricted to the bathroom and kitchen, but in the farmhouse and villa gardens of Tuscany, water appears in several guises – in basins, fountains, ponds

OPPOSITE

Following on from the legacy left by the ancient Romans, Renaissance architects also built aqueducts, which were often used as a means of feeding the water gardens of Tuscan villas.

RIGHT

Water is an essential part of the Tuscan landscape, and has been a desired feature of the garden since ancient times, when the Romans in Tuscany laid out their gardens with fountains, canals, ponds and pools.

and pools. Any one or all of these are typical features of the garden, and often take a central role in the layout and design of the landscaping. A small formal garden may be arranged around a single fountain of stone or marble, and the sound of cascading water becomes a sensory feature in itself. In combination with pathways paved with *cotto* bricks, gravel or pebbles, lemon trees in terracotta pots, box hedges or jasmine vines, and the stone basin of the fountain itself, the inclusion of water creates a complete environment. Every element of nature is represented.

Alternatively, a rustic farmhouse garden might be arranged on more informal lines, with fewer formal plantings other than perhaps some vines, and fruit or olive trees. Geraniums in terracotta pots add colour, while basil, rosemary, sage and thyme (planted in pots or in beds) keep the kitchen supplied with essential herbs. In this setting, the water element may be an ancient stone basin, once used to water the livestock that lived in the farmhouse in ages past but now stocked with a few fish or planted with water lilies.

A variation on the simple, functional basin is the wall-mounted garden *badia*, which in ancient times provided a source of drinking water, but is now largely decorative. This type of aquatic ornamentation is found in many Tuscan gardens and comes in numerous forms, from a simple stone basin on the wall of a farmhouse yard to a sculptural head spouting water from its mouth into a basin or pond below. The variety of these sculptured fountain spouts is truly incredible, and ranges from a lion's head to the masks of gods, monsters and mythical creatures. They are made in terracotta, in marble and in stone, and can help to bring the aesthetics of the fantastical grotto into one corner of a simple garden. This tradition of decorative fountain faucets and fixtures has a history spanning centuries.

ABOVE & RIGHT

Mountain streams spill out into the main Tuscan rivers – in particular
the Arno and its tributaries Cecina, Ombrone and Albegna – which wind
their way down through hill towns, valleys and villages on course for
the Mar Tirreno, the Tyhrrenian Sea. These waterways are the source
of brown river trout, a delicacy of the alpine area.

One of the oldest and most favoured Tuscan symbols is the lion – the lion's head has been consistently used in garden sculpture since Roman times, and lion's paws also appear as details in fountain sculpture as well as furniture. Animals were extremely popular motifs for the garden in the late Renaissance, when a renewed interest in the mysteries of nature triggered a fascination for the world of living creatures. This expanded to encompass animal-like inventions from mythology, and imaginative creations that were part animal, part human.

A keen interest in the realm of mythology also unleashed a vogue for stone and marble masks used as fountains. These expressionistic masks depicted macabre and contorted faces with wild, wide-eyed looks. These old masks can still be uncovered at flea markets, but more usually are reproduced by stonemasons and potters for inclusion in the private walled garden of the villa.

Some of the grandest villas and castles in Tuscany boast water features that have survived for centuries and been restored in recent times. Until modern water supply and piping came to Tuscany, most properties of any size had a stone water reservoir – in essence, a large square or rectangular pool – to supply the household as well as the garden. An ancient reservoir dating from the early Renaissance, or even an aqueduct in the form of a deep, stone-lined canal running through the grounds, is a wonderfully historic feature that in some cases can be adapted to more hedonistic ends, as a place for swimming or as a fish pond.

One water element of the Tuscan garden that cannot be ignored is the swimming pool. Although it is thought of today as a modern incursion into traditional architecture and landscaping, the notion of a pool for swimming and bathing has venerable origins. Swimming was a popular pastime in the days of ancient Rome, and pools and outdoor baths were included in the gardens of the wealthy for this purpose.

It is really only since the twentieth century that swimming as a health-giving pursuit became popularised, and modern construction technology enabled pools to be built far more easily and economically. The swimming pool has become the quintessential accessory of the Tuscan villa, a sign of leisure and luxury. Usually situated at the back of the villa, away from public view, the Tuscan swimming pool is more than just a place to cool off. Much consideration is given to the aesthetics of the pool, the materials used to build it and its situation in relation to the house and surrounding countryside.

In its positioning, the pool is intended to blend seamlessly with the textures and mood of the house and gardens. It is sometimes screened by rows of tall cypress trees, blocking the strong afternoon sun or softening chilly evening breezes. However, the pool is designed and located primarily to take advantage of views of the surrounding countryside. The eye of the onlooker is meant to follow the length of the pool, to vistas of golden fields where hay dries in the hot sun, or to rolling hills dotted with farmhouses and villas, or down sloping terraces planted with vines or olive trees.

The design of the swimming pool is aimed at creating an unobtrusive and artless appearance. Modern or experimental shapes are shunned in favour of a classic rectangle, and ceramic tiling is minimised. A rough-textured terracotta tile usually provides a subtle rim for the pool, with stone flagging or terracotta brick extending beyond. In fact, often the edge of the pool is flush with the ground rather than finished with a raised surround, therefore evoking a more naturalistic mood and allowing the pool to disappear into its environment. There is nothing to draw undue attention to the pool, other than the play of sunlight on the water's surface. The integrity and harmony of the garden are maintained – a typically Tuscan approach. In other settings a swimming pool is a status symbol to be flaunted and enhanced with all manner of decorative flourishes, but in the heartland of Tuscany the pool is given an earthy and rustic treatment.

Water was once far more difficult to supply to country dwellings, which might have been positioned far away from natural sources such as rivers and streams. Well-to-do Renaissance country dwellers might install aqueducts and reservoirs, but up until the late twentieth century, the primary source of water for most farmhouses was the stone well, which was a purely functional piece of construction. (Now, however, such wells are often filled in, or occasionally have been restored to make a garden feature.) For those that could afford it, the fountain was the preferred source of water: with its running stream, it provided a more hygienic source, without the worry of stagnation. The fountains that have so beautifully enhanced the gardens and courtyards of Tuscan houses for over two thousand years have utilitarian origins. In ancient Rome, and in many of its colonies, a great system of aqueducts fed fountains situated in public squares as well as in private townhouses and villas. By medieval times the fountain had all but disappeared from architecture and the urban setting, but in the Renaissance period the fountain was revived.

In Renaissance cities, the public fountain was the focal point of town life. In the days before water was connected to every house, citizens collected their water from fountains in the main piazzas. In the case of a hilltop city such as Siena, public fountains were served by aqueducts bringing water from the hills. Maintaining and constructing the aqueducts and fountains was an important task of local government. In the thirteenth century, for example, a number of old fountains were rebuilt and new ones constructed in order to ensure an adequate supply of water for the growing population. As the Renaissance continued, the aesthetics of the urban environment became increasingly important and the most prominent fountains were transformed into spectacular showcases of civic pride. Master sculptors were commissioned

RIGHT

A large man-made reservoir is the centrepiece of the wine-growing
estate of Tenuta di Trinoro, situated above the Val d'Orcia. In the hot
summer months the water feature provides a pleasing outloook from
the villa, and harmonises beautifully with walls built in part from local
river stone.

to make centrepieces for the main urban fountains. The idea of the fountain as a decorative device naturally made its way into the private setting of the villa, and even the least pretentious villa installed a fountain as the focal point of the garden. In those homes owned by wealthy aristocrats and merchants, fountains were adorned with sculpture; indeed, a fountain in the garden is still very much a part of the Tuscan country house.

These days fountains no longer serve any great practical purpose, and exist purely for the appreciation of the viewer. If a fountain is particularly beautiful (made from marble or featuring sculptural elements), it becomes an object of admiration. But even if it is only simple in design – perhaps a plain stone basin set against the garden wall, with a small spout from which clear water trickles – the fountain is still a soothing and comforting presence, especially in summer. Its sound can be heard from anywhere in the garden, from the terrace or within the house.

The value of water for decorative as well as utilitarian functions can be traced clearly to ancient Roman times, when the ideas and patterns laid out for the use of water – in particular, the use of water in the garden – were first formalized. The garden was intended as a sensuous place where nature could be tamed for enjoyment, and water was one of its chief components.

Pliny the Younger's descriptions of his villa in Tuscany give valuable first-hand insight into how water was employed in the Roman garden. 'Water flows from a marble basin, and by its gentle sprinkling nourishes both the planes, and what grows under them,' he said in a letter to Apollinaris. And again: 'a small fountain, with a basin, round which the playing of several small pipes makes a most agreeable murmuring'. In yet another part of the garden, Pliny wrote of baths and a cold plunge pool, 'but if you are inclined to swim more at large or warm, in the area is a piscina and near it a conveyance of water, from where you may again close the pores when you think the heat too great'.

OPPOSITE & ABOVE

The hot spa waters of Tuscany have lured visitors since ancient Roman times when imperial army officers took rest and recreation at resorts such as Bagni di Lucca. Other spas, or terme, *include Montecatini with its Art Nouveau buildings, Bagni Vignoni, which has an ancient hot pool in the centro of the village, and Saturnia with its cascades of hot water.*

Pliny described at least five fountains with moving water, in addition to the baths and pools for bathing and swimming. His letters, along with other Classical documents, were a huge source of inspiration to early Renaissance garden designers and villa builders. At this time, the use of water in the garden was intended less for enjoyment and more for spiritual and intellectual reasons. In both art and architecture, the garden was envisaged as symbolising the biblical Garden of Eden. It was typically arranged in a square, with a tree or spring placed in the centre representing Christ, and four streams (representing the four Evangelists) flowing north, south, east and west to form a cross.

The early Renaissance garden, however, was still essentially practical in nature, following on from its purpose in medieval times as a place for growing food for the household. Adjoining orchards and vegetable plantings was a small plot of ground comprising ornamental parterres, paths, orange and lemon trees in terracotta pots, perhaps some fragrant or medicinal herbs. It might also have included a modest water feature – a small stone or marble fountain, or even an ornamental fish pond.

However, as the Renaissance progressed the idea of the garden as a place for enjoyment and spiritual refreshment took hold, and water played a greater role in the layout and landscaping of outdoor areas. This concept continues to hold sway in the villa gardens of the present day, for water is thought to add a cooling dimension to the garden as well as nourishing the spirit. The tinkling sound of a garden fountain, the sight of water shimmering in a sunlit pond, is uplifting and soothing. And it is the application of water for these secondary purposes that is so beautifully executed in traditional Tuscan building.

The Islamic influences that reached Tuscany in the thirteenth and fourteenth centuries had a profound effect on the attitude towards water in the garden. An interest in the Classical myths, art and poetry was revived. The medieval fountain came to represent both the elemental forces and earthly pleasures of nature, and gardens were designed with references to Classical scenes and text that only the educated aristocrat could recognize. In the form of grottoes,

RIGHT

An ancient bath is enclosed by an impressive vaulted ceiling constructed from brick. The practice of bathing in health-giving spa waters has long formed a part of Tuscan culture and lifestyle.

waterfalls and nymphaea (a type of pavillion with fountains and statues), nature was presented as though in the wild, yet with the all-important connection to Classical culture.

Those householders who could not afford such extravagances might follow the fashion on a smaller scale, with a fountain and Classical statue in a courtyard rather than a grotto. Significantly, by the end of the Renaissance the inclusion of a water feature was irrevocably set in garden design. Greenery and water were dominant features of the Tuscan garden, becoming more important than either stone or marble.

The trend of including water elements in Tuscan gardens was largely inspired by Renaissance writers. Francesco di Giorgio thought the garden should incorporate 'fish ponds, loggias, covered and open walks, and places … with water courses'. Giovanni Boccaccio, author of the fourteenth-century *Decameron*, described an idealistic scenario in the villa garden in which water plays an allegorical role, symbolising regeneration and purification. He wrote of a villa, 'surrounded by meadows and wondrous gardens where fountains of the coolest water flowed', including one fountain 'of the whitest marble with marvellous inlay work' and crowned with a 'statue borne upon a column'.

As the Renaissance progressed, the religious certainties and dominant humanist philosophy (in which human beings were placed at the centre of the universe) broke down. The subsequent emphasis on the natural world, and its relationship with the man-made world, made the garden increasingly more important. The next phase in landscape design – the Mannerist garden – began in the late sixteenth century. The challenging and experimental spirit of

LEFT & RIGHT

A simple, terracotta-edged swimming pool is a natural extension of the patio. Its rustic look blends with the rest of the house, which was built from scratch, incorporating building materials that were reclaimed from old farmhouses and villas.

Mannerism led to the transformation of the garden, from its relatively small size and philosophically derived layout and features, to a place of amusement and theatricality, designed to impress and entertain visitors.

While the villa exterior remained austere and Classical in its design and execution, the garden became a creative arena. This was a realm in which nature was subverted; where the human manipulation of natural forces could be explored. Artifice was the prevailing characteristic, and how better to demonstrate the submission of nature than through the control of water, the most precious and elusive of natural resources? Fish ponds, grottoes and water theatres became important components of the garden and, given that many villas were situated on hilltops (or at least on high ground), gardens were designed to take advantage of the natural slope of the land. These terraced gardens often included waterfalls and watercourses that splashed from one level to the next.

Some villas incorporated quite spectacular displays of water. The Medici villa at Castello was named after the Roman aqueduct running from Florence to Sesto Fiorentino that also fed the villa's elaborate water gardens. The territory of the garden was conceived as a metaphor for the political realm of the Medici family. At the top of the garden was a water reservoir crowned by a bronze statue personifying the Apennines, the source of Tuscany's rivers. The reservoir supplied a series of canals, which were interspersed with fountains illustrating Tuscan mountains and rivers. The canals finished their course with two more fountains in the main garden, which also featured a grotto filled with animal sculptures and fountains.

Consider the impression the garden had on Michel de Montaigne (writing in 1580):

'We went to look at the principal fountain, which discharges its contents through two large figures in bronze, the lower of which has taken the other in his arms, and is squeezing him with all his might ... There is also a very handsome grotto, in which are to be seen all sorts of animals, sculptured the size of life, which are spouting out water, some by the beak, others by the mouth, or the nails, or the nostrils.'

At the Medici villa at Pratolino, nature was again tamed to serve the amusement of the villa owners and their guests. Michel de Montaigne admired this grotto also:

'Here you see various musical instruments which perform a variety of pieces, by the agency of the water, which also, by a hidden machinery, gives motion to several statues, single and in groups, opens doors, and gives apparent animation to the figures of various animals, that seem to jump into the water, to drink, to swim about, and so on.'

To effect such impressive waterworks, as well as a dazzling sequence of waterfalls and pools, the villa at Pratolino was fed by a 5km (3 mile) aqueduct. Today there are only a few extant reminders of the fantastic water features that reached their pinnacle in the Mannerist period of the late sixteenth century and continued to be popular in the Baroque age of the seventeenth century.

The secret sunken garden at Villa Torrigiani, near Lucca, was conceived as a source of amusement for the owners (the Santini family) and their guests. Visitors would descend the stairs of the sunken walled garden to find themselves trapped by a wall of water shooting up from fountains hidden at the top of the stairs and from the pebble mosaics along the whole garden. If they sought refuge in the grotto at the far end of the garden, a series of waterworks issuing from the mouths of the grotto's statues sent them running again. Their escape route back up to the terrace was marked by a statue of the nymph Flora that would shower them with water.

The Boboli Gardens are the most famous example of Mannerist garden design, and include several grottoes as well as a series of beautiful fountains and waterspouts fashioned as an array of fantastical creatures. The fountains, with their control and display of water sprays, were proof of nature harnessed.

The grottoes, meanwhile, explored the realms of imagination and mysticism, using water in the form of jets and hydraulics to provoke the emotions and surprise the viewer. Such elaborate water theatre is no longer fashionable, and there are few legacies of these artificial constructs today. In modern times Tuscan gardens have returned to their original fourteenth-century ideal: small, restful places where the sound of water provides an essential aid to calm and quiet relaxation. Water is again valued as a spiritual element.

However, these days the water feature of the garden is not the theological symbol of regeneration and purification that it was in Roman and early Renaissance times. Instead, the villa owner appreciates water for its sensual qualities: the sound of water and its cool spray, its rippling, light-reflective surface, all help to erase the concerns of the day and revive the simple pleasures of nature. Climate is also an important consideration when it comes to the use of water in the region's gardens. Tuscan summers are long and intense, and a pool of water is a refreshing inclusion for outdoor areas. Where there is no room for a swimming pool, a small pond or fountain can alleviate the stifling midday heat and bring a sense of relief.

The significance of water as a reviving, health-giving element is not lost in Tuscany, which has a venerable tradition of 'taking the waters' at thermal spas (terme). In the northwest of the region, spas fed by volcanic water sources have been visited in the pursuit of good health since ancient Roman times. Montecatini (at the foot of the Pistoian Mountains) and nearby Bagni de Lucca are the best-known Tuscan hot springs: these were used by Roman soldiers on leave, and became popular with royalty during the Middle Ages.

ABOVE

There are few sights more inviting on midsummer Tuscan days than a shimmering expanse of cool water, edged with sun-warmed stone and pots of bright pink geraniums, a poolside lounger and a crisp white canvas sun umbrella.

RIGHT

In Renaissance times, a steeply sloping site was turned to advantage with water gardens arranged over stepped terraces. In modern times, hilly terrain has been just as cleverly adapted. Here, a long lap pool perches high above the valley below.

Both Montecatini and Bagni de Lucca began developing as resorts in the eighteenth century, when drainage techniques enabled the natural waters to be contained and manipulated into a formalised spa environment. At Montecatini, King Leopoldo I commissioned the architect Gaspare Paoletti to build the Neoclassical baths of Leopoldino and the Terme Tettuccio in the style of Imperial Rome. Before the end of the century, a hospital and the first hotel had also been built. However, it was not until the early decades of the twentieth century that Montecatini became one of the most fashionable European spa resorts.

A number of luxury hotels and baths were built in lavish Art Nouveau style and attracted an elite list of guests, including royalty from Russia and eastern Europe. Giuseppe Verdi famously visited the spa for twenty-five years in search of eternal youth. The thermal springs certainly have a reputation for their curative benefits, and those in search of regeneration continue to come to Montecatini to drink the water and immerse themselves at one of the nine terme.

To the north-east, not far from the town of Lucca, the spa resort of Bagni de Lucca attracts visitors to its many thermal cures. They follow in the footsteps of royals, aristocrats and writers of the early nineteenth century, when the spa was in its heyday. Victor Hugo, Flaubert, Shelley, Byron, Fanny Trollope, and Elizabeth and Robert Browning were among those who came to stroll the chestnut alleys and take the steam treatments and mud baths. Like the wealthy inhabitants of Florence, they came here as much for the cool mountain air and leafy scenery as for the waters. Bagni de Lucca remains a refreshing escape from the sweltering summer heat that beats down on the Tuscan plains, and the rushing waters of the Lima River still dominate the quiet town.

The waters of the coast gradually proved more of a lure than the thermal springs of the mountains – a trend that began in the late 1800s and gained pace through the twentieth century. Along the coast of Versilia, a formal beach culture has evolved between Forte dei Marmi to the north and Torre del Lago Puccini in the south. The 20 km (12 mile) sliver of coast is interspersed with pine groves and sandy beaches, where the bold blue-and-white-striped

RIGHT

A stone basin, affixed to a garden wall, spills over into a small, still pool which once would have provided the household with water for cooking and washing.

BELOW

In the Tuscan garden surprising finds can be made in unlikely places. Set into a stone wall made from large irregular stones, a shiny brass faucet shoots water amongst the fallen autumn leaves that have collected in the basin below.

ABOVE

As always, the trick in Tuscan garden design is to make contrived elements seem completely natural. Water channels made of stone, or of terracotta, have historically been common devices for sending a trickle of water cascading throughout the garden.

—

OPPOSITE

In a natural, almost wild, corner of a garden, a crumbling old stone fountain takes on the appearance of some primitive, long-forgotten monument. Partly overgrown with foliage, it pours forth into a small pond.

umbrellas of bathing establishments, or bagni, have become a signature motif. Viarreggio – with its Art Deco cafes and rows of recliners and umbrellas marking out the sand – was the first beach resort in Italy. It remains to this day an elegant example of how the Tuscans tamed the beachside and turned sea bathing into a gracious exercise.

In contrast with the ordered lines of bagni stretching along the Versilian riviera, the Maremma coast to the south is wild and mysterious. The water of the Mediterranean Sea is at its most beautiful – clean, shimmering and transparent blue – lapping the rocky perimeter of the Parco Naturale della Maremma. The fragrant scrub runs right down to the sea, sometimes clinging to edge of sheer cliffs and at other times sharing the salty rocks with seagulls.

From the peaceful cliff-top fishing village of Talamone, the coast sweeps down to the Argentario peninsula. Once part of the Tuscan archipelago, but now separated from the mainland except for three narrow spits of land, Monte Argentario and the neighbouring islands of Giannutri and Giglio are beautifully scenic and untamed. Roads and coastal paths wind around rocky coves, inlets and bays, while in the clear sea waters, yachts and fishing boats meander on their way back to the harbours of Porto San Stefano or Port' Ercole. Far from the August heat of Florence and the central plains, this stretch of Mediterranean seashore offers a distinctively Tuscan interpretation of the beach resort. Echoing the unpretentious tone of Tuscany's rustic architecture and gardens, the marine culture on the coast is charmingly naive.

Just as water in the villa garden gives off a cooling mist and lulls the senses with its gentle murmuring, the water of the sea has a powerful allure that draws Tuscans on sunny summer days. They live here in the same style as they do in their pastoral farmhouses and villas: fusing tradition and history with a lively appreciation for the present; balancing the austerely rustic with the luxuriant; and relishing the intrinsic beauty of natural elements such as stone, wood, earth and water. Above all, the Tuscan approach is to find ways of harnessing these natural elements to construct an inspired environment, and then to shape that environment to make the experiences of everyday living that little bit more refined.

ABOVE

The public water source was the focal point of village life in Tuscany up until the early twentieth century: (from left) an ornamented well at Pienza; a simpler affair at Empoli; and a washing basin, or vasce, *with channels to drain the water.*

OPPOSITE

A historic marble well at the village of San Quirico d'Orcia, south of Siena, is capped by a streamlined yet graceful wrought-iron arch embellished with swirling brackets. It supports an iron bucket on a chain that can be lowered to collect water.

LEFT

Set against a bank of flowers, this Neoclassical fountain, edged with stone spheres, is fed by

a natural spring in use since Etruscan times.

ABOVE LEFT & RIGHT

The realms of fantasy were explored by Tuscan garden designers and architects of the sixteenth

century. Their gardens were populated by exotic creatures and magical, metaphysical

elements rendered in stone and marble, creating a visual tension between art and nature.

Such ideas have continued to influence garden design.

BELOW

The plainest of water features takes on a utilitarian beauty when rendered as simply and unpretentiously as this. The rugged and unsophisticated nature of the stone wall contrasts with the smooth, symmetrical, cut-stone basin fixed below.

RIGHT

A wide terracotta 'mouth' is set in a rough stone wall, chanelling water from one part of the garden to another. This technique was made popular in Renaissance landscape design as a way of moving water throughout the garden, regardless of the terrain.

OPPOSITE

Embellishment of the streetscape is an important element in defining the individual character and visual style of Tuscany's villages and towns. For centuries, a strong sense of civic pride has been expressed through elegant public facilities such as fountains, wells and faucets, which serve a noble purpose.

ABOVE

The aesthetic legacy of the Renaissance is evident in even the smallest details of Tuscan civic architecture, in public squares and streets. The humble water faucet is transformed into an object of beauty and imagination, whether in the form of a gryphon, a bird in flight, or a grotesque mask.

glossary

ALABASTER fine-grained type of limestone, white or yellowish white with a translucent appearance. Mined by the Etruscans in Central Italy, and was subsequently used in the Middle Ages, particularly for the tracery of church windows.

ATRIUM an inner courtyard

BATTISCOPA skirting board edging interior walls, usually made from wood or terracotta

BRECCIA DI SERAVEZZA deep-violet marble displaying fragments of white, pink and pale green marble, quarried at Stratzema, near Seravezza. Popularly used for the tops of tables, as well as for the pedestals of sculptures.

BROCATELLE DE SIENNE dark violet marble with orange spots, quarried at Marmière

CARRARINO name given to marble from the quarries of Carrara, in the Apuan Alps

CASA COLONICA farmhouse, traditional home of the farmer, or agent, managing the landowner's estate. They are typically block-shaped, with a sloping terracotta-tiled roof and dovecote.

CASSEPANCA a long bench with a back and hinged seat that lifted to reveal storage space underneath

CASSETTE garden box or basin, usually fashioned in terracotta and often featuring relief decoration

CASETTE A SCHIERE a terrace of small, upright workers' houses, typical of the Tuscan hill towns

CASSONE wooden storage chest with a hinged lid; one of the most common items of furniture in the Renaissance. Made in three forms: a simple rectangle; convex (boat-shaped); or contoured (like a sarcophagus).

COPPI semi-circular terracotta tile used for roofing

CORTILE an inner courtyard with arcading

COTTÒ terracotta bricks or tiles used for flooring

CORNICE ornamental moulding that projects along the top of a building, wall or arch, to serve as a finished edge to the structure

CREDENZA cupboard typical of the Renaissance, characterised by symmetrical placement of drawers and cupboards and architectural-style mouldings. Base was often supported by four carved animal feet.

DANTE one of the main types of chair of the 15th century in Italy. A folding chair featuring X-shaped legs, based on an earlier Roman model.

DOVECOTE (or **COLOMBAIA**) a tower, or chimney-like structure, used to keep pigeons, traditionally for consumption by the household

FRIEZE band that runs below the cornice along an interior wall, usually with a decorated surface; the band that sits between the architrave and the cornice on an exterior wall

GALESTRO a coarse, Impruneta clay high in iron, copper, calcium, and aluminium, enabling the fired product to withstand temperatures as cold as -30C.

GROTTO an artificial cave, or cavern, decorated with rock and shell work, and typically with water elements and sculptures. First recorded as a feature of ancient Roman gardens and was revived in the Renaissance to become widely used in the Tuscan gardens of grand villas and palazzos.

IMPRUNETA Tuscan town renowned for its production of terracotta since Renaissance times, when local kiln artisans made the tiles used by architect Bruneschelli for the dome of Florence cathedral. The unique chemical composition of the clay, coupled with high firing temperatures, produce what is considered the only true frost-proof terracotta.

INTARSIA inlay technique in which shaped three-dimensional pieces of inlay material (usually wood) are set into a hollowed-out space in the ground

LAVELLO wall-mounted basins with taps, for the garden

LOGGIA room or gallery that is open to the outdoors on one or more sides

MAJOLICA (or maiolica as it is also known) type of tin-glazed earthenware, in which the fired clay is coated with tin glaze to create a white background on which colours can then be applied for decoration, usually blue, yellow, orange, brown and green. The finished surface is shiny and glassy. Majolica is used for tableware, as well as tiles.

MARQUETRY veneer-like inlay technique in which flat pieces of material, such as wood, ivory and shell, are fitted together to create a continuous surface

MISCHIO DI SERAVEZZA deep-violet marble with clouds of pink, from Seravezza; used widely by the Medici grand dukes for their monuments in Florence during the 16th century

MOBILI RUSTICI rustic furniture, usually of the 16th, 17th and 18th centuries. Particularly sought-after are wooden chests (*cassepanca*) and Savonarola and Dante chairs

MONTARENTI marble quarry near Sienna noted for its black-veined marbles

ORCIO urn, or pitcher with a narrow mouth.

PALAZZO an urban 'palace'; a grand residence.

PENSILE hanging garden, arranged in terraces on a steeply sloping site. Terraces are contained by retaining walls and linked by monumental staircases, such as at Villa Torrigiani, Lucca.

PIETRA FORTE an arenacious limestone traditionally quarried in the hills around Florence

PIETRA SERENA variety of calcerous, soft grey sandstone found north of Florence on the southern slopes of the Apennines

PORTICO a roofed entrance to a building that serves as the focal point of the façade; often incorporating columns and a pediment

QUOINS dressed stone used at the corners of buildings; usually laid with alternating large and small blocks

SAVONAROLA a folding chair popular in the 15th century. Constructed from a series of interlaced wooden staves, with a low shaped back and armrests, both of which were usually decorated with carving or inlay.

SIENNA BROCATELLO yellowish marble with numerous interlaced veins

STATUARIO high-quality marble reserved for sculpture

STUCCO slow-setting plaster used for rendering internal and external walls; primarily made up of gypsum, sand and slaked lime. Developed by the ancient Romans.

TASCA semi-circular terracotta wall containers that are typically ridged or scalloped or festooned with a garland.

TEGOLA a flat terracotta tile used for roofing. In the style developed by the Romans, it is placed directly on the pitched roof structure and then topped with two semi-circular tiles, called *coppi*.

TERRACOTTA from the Italian meaning baked earth, any kind of fired, unglazed pottery. In general usage refers

to an object made from a coarse, porous clay that takes on a rich red-gold hue when fired.

TERRA TURCHINA characteristic clay of the pottery town of Impruneta; produces a terracotta that is extremely durable, resistant to frost and temperature changes

TERRAZZO type of flooring developed by the Romans; marble chips are mixed with concrete and poured into the floor space, then ground and polished to take on a high shine.

TUFA porous grey volcanic stone used for building, particularly by the ancient Romans

TUSCAN ORDER style of column, as classified by the Roman architect and scholar Vitruvius. One of four types of column; the simplest one, with a smooth, cylindrical shaft - apparently reflecting its origins in the wooden temples of the Etruscans.

VASO garden pot in a vase-like shape, with a wide mouth tapering in size to the base. Typically made from terracotta, variations include *vaso liscio*, with a double border around the pot, or *vaso festonato*, decorated with a garland.

VILLA-FATTORIA manor house, home of the country estate owner – from the 15th century onwards usually a member of the rising bourgeoisie. Also known as the *villa signorille*, *villa padronale* or *casa di signore*, sometimes built from scratch, but more often an expanded and embellished dwelling based on a medieval tower house, or on the farmhouse formerly inhabited by the landowner's agent.

index

acknowledgements

The author would like to thank the staff at Co & Bear, especially David Shannon and Pritty Ramjee, for their patience and goodwill. Special thanks to Bradd Nicholls, Daisy Nicholls, Emma Saunders and Lizzie Terry for their kindness and support. The publishers would like to thank all the owners who have kindly let us publish images of their houses for this book. We have always tried to obtain permission for use, please accept our apologies if this has not always been possible. With special thanks to Sue Townsend of Palazzo Terranova, who generously allowed us to use the images on pages 10-11, 28-29, 164-165 and 126-127, (tel: +39 (0) 75 857 0083, www.palazzoterranova.com).